letters of light for
first ladies

letters of light for
first ladies

CECELIA WILLIAMS BRYANT

Kathryn V. Stanley, editor

JUDSON PRESS
PUBLISHERS SINCE 1824
VALLEY FORGE, PA

Bible quotations in this volume are from the following versions:
The New Revised Standard Version (NRSV), copyright © 1989, 1995 by the Division of Christian Education of the National Council of the Churches of Christ in the United States of America. Used by permission. All rights reserved.
Contemporary English Version (CEV), copyright © 1995 by American Bible Society. Used by permission.
New King James Version (NKJV), copyright © 1982 by Thomas Nelson, Inc. Used by permission. All rights reserved.
The Holy Bible, New Century Version® (NCV), copyright © 2005 by Thomas Nelson, Inc.
Holy Bible, New Living Translation (NLT), copyright © 1996, 2004 by Tyndale Charitable Trust. Used by permission of Tyndale House Publishers.
The Holy Bible, King James Version (KJV).
HOLY BIBLE: New International Version (NIV), copyright © 1973, 1978, 1984. Used by permission of Zondervan Bible Publishers.
The New American Standard Bible (NASB), © 1960, 1962, 1963, 1968, 1971, 1972, 1973, 1975, 1977 by The Lockman Foundation. Used by permission.

Library of Congress Cataloging-in-Publication Data

Bryant, Cecelia Williams.
    Letters of light for first ladies / Cecelia Williams Bryant ; Kathryn V. Stanley, editor. — 1st ed.
        p. cm.
    ISBN 978-0-8170-1527-5 (pbk. : alk. paper) 1. Spouses of clergy—Religious life. 2. Spouses of clergy—Conduct of life. 3. Wives—Religious life. 4. Wives—Conduct of life. I. Stanley, Kathryn V. II. Title.

    BV4395.B79 2007
    248.8'92—dc22

                                                                            2007035210

Printed on recycled paper in the U.S.A.
First printing, 2008.

Because you allowed me to drink deeply and frequently
from the well of your faith.
Because you covered the nakedness of my pain
with your compassion and hope.
Because you ignited my soul with songs of glory,
power, and beauty.
Because you opened my eyes to a cosmos
of revelation and mystery.
Because I never had to wonder if I was alone,
forgotten, unapproved, or lost.
Because I found light in your light, God in your wisdom,
and love in your voice.
Because eternity is never far away when I think of you.
Because you made sense out of the chaos of religion.
Because you drew a circle of prayer around my destiny.
Because you manifested holy matrimony.

Because you love my children.
Because you don't hold my faults against me.
Because I am liberated by your encouragement.
My gratitude to you,
Lady Phyliss Naomi Hurly Davis
and
Dr. Sylvia Ross Talbot
for being exemplars of light as clergy spouses.

And to our daughter-in-love,
Giselle Annette Graves Bryant,
who makes my life more centered, more radiant by the
magnitude of her compassion,
the light of her wisdom, and the depth of her soul.

The true light, which enlightens everyone.
(John 1:9, NRSV)

Contents

FOREWORD

First Lady

Blessed is the one who reads aloud the words of
the prophecy, and blessed are those who hear and
who keep what is written in it; for the time is near.
(Revelation 1:3, NRSV)

The journey of a first lady is often a venture into unchartered, undocumented, and previously unknown territory. It is a journey filled with the unexpected and the unexplained, where often one experiences the highest of highs and the lowest of lows. It is a journey that all too often one experiences alone and in isolation, without the benefit of a shoulder to lean on or a sounding board to vent.

There is no roadmap for this journey, just OJT—on-the-journey training. There are land mines, pitfalls, and carcasses at every turn, and only those who have a true relationship with God and great mentors along the way are able to survive and thrive. Rev. Dr. Cecelia Williams Bryant is one of those mentors. She is someone who has successfully completed her OJT, gotten the diploma, and bought the t-shirt. She is a mentor who not only understands how to survive and thrive but also knows how essential it is to "become." Rev. C, as she is affectionately known, is the trailblazer for those of us who have opted not to choose the path of least resistance but rather to proudly embrace who we were created to be.

Helping first ladies "become" everything that God has created us to be is a major part of Rev. C's ministry. Her ministry in many ways represents to first ladies what Harriet Tubman's ministry represented to the slaves: *freedom*. Her ministry represents freedom to break away from conventional thinking and the traditional norms of ministerial life and congregational expectations. It represents freedom and the right to have a life and a ministry apart from the ministers to whom we are married. Her ministry represents freedom to walk beside and not three feet behind our husbands. Her ministry represents freedom to "become."

I am personally thankful to Rev. C for her ministry to first ladies because it has had a profound and lasting impact on my life. My personality, as it is, clearly does not fit into the first lady stereotype. I rarely wear hats. I don't have the patience of Job, nor do I have the enduring sweetness of Mary. I am, for all intents and purposes, a misfit, a first lady who did not seem to fit in anywhere. Nonetheless, Rev. C helped me to create a personal space and a personal expression that is unashamedly and uniquely me. Because of Rev. C, I now have the opportunity to help other seeming misfits find their place and space.

There are many benefactors of Rev. C's first ladies' ministry, and we all feel truly blessed and thankful for her place in our lives. She is a mother/sister/friend, she is a grandmother to our children, she is a mother-in-love to our husbands, and a confidant and counselor to all. I have never known anyone with such unlimited space in her heart and in her life for God's people as Rev. C. She fills an uncommon space in this world, which is why I am so happy she has written *Letters of Light for First Ladies*.

In writing *Letters of Light for First Ladies*, Rev. C has wholeheartedly embraced the opportunity to reach first ladies all over the globe who need encouragement, an understanding ear, and, most important, nonjudgmental love. This book will serve to inspire and ignite those who have caved in under the pressure to conform and those who have lost the will to "become." It will transform long-held paradigms and refocus our energies. Most important, it will bring us back to ourselves, which also means bringing us back to God. What more could we ask?

Thank you, Rev. C, for your out-of-the-box thinking, your courageous spirit, your unwavering conviction, and most of all your steadfast dedication to God and his people, particularly first ladies. On behalf of your mentees and first ladies everywhere, thank you for the time, energy, and prayer spent in birthing this book. Thank you for sharing your own journey of "becoming" and for being a pioneer for those of us who will follow. Last, thank you for helping us to understand that "there is enough room in the sky for all the stars to shine." First ladies everywhere, let's embrace our opportunity to shine!

Denise Brown Hunter
First Lady
First African Methodist Episcopal Church
Los Angeles, California

Acknowledgments

For we do not wrestle against flesh and blood,
but against principalities, against powers,
against the rulers of the darkness of this age,
against spiritual hosts of wickedness in the heavenly places.
(Ephesians 6:12, NKJV)

The exceedingly great warfare that has been waged in the process of writing and publishing a book about this ministry exposes how great the assault is on clergy family life. How death-defying we must be every time we seek to fulfill our prophetic purposes.

My heart is ablaze with thanksgiving for the ministering angels assigned to keep me: the comfort and strength of my incredible husband, John, who treats me like a queen; the Healing Rooms of Spokane, Washington, under the direction of Cal and Michelle Pierce; and the mighty saints of God who intercede for me daily.

Most of all, I am thankful for the clergy spouses who for nearly forty years have shared with me their hearts, their hurts, and their hopes.

May God bless us all.

Prologue

Marriage is a covenant relationship ordained by God. Yet it is as mundane as it is divine. While every covenant marriage is shaped by the light of Scripture, under the best of circumstances marriage is one of the most difficult tasks that any man or woman undertakes.

Marriages where one spouse is a clergyperson have special challenges as well as special graces. If one or both of you perceive the relationship as superspiritual, the mundane is oft-times neglected, if not ignored. Sooner or later, this will have tragic results.

So often clergy spouses attempt to navigate the realms of the mystery of matrimony believing and expecting that their marriages, indeed, their entire lives are or should be lived without spot or blemish. Forcing themselves to suffer in silence, they struggle to survive without the benefit of healthy intervention. For this reason, many clergy spouses feel isolated, vulnerable, put upon, frustrated, or empty. And the fruit of bitterness is chaos.

Yet, because God is faithful, many clergy marriages not only appear successful, they really are successful. But even the favor of God includes lamentation. The clergy spouse who seeks to walk in the light of God is all too familiar with what the medieval mystic St. John of the Cross called "the dark night of the soul," that desolate and lonely place in life that may result in a deeper and closer walk with God, a place that has the capacity to stretch and sanctify us through very real personal suffering. But in the meantime, if the clergy spouse who carries the world on his or her shoulders has chosen to live a myth or a stereotype, this will only sap his or her strength. Nevertheless, if we choose life, if we embrace God's light, despite life's struggles, we are ultimately sustained by the knowledge that we are created for God's love. In the economy of heaven, there is more than enough love for each of us.

That divine knowledge has undergirded my marriage for nearly forty years. God has set me free from panic attacks, depression, acute loneliness, and deep sorrow. Our marriage has endured the financial stress of the early years of our ministry in New England, the tumult and deterioration of the quality of family life in inner-city Baltimore, a coup in Liberia during our service there as Episcopal leaders, the exhaustion of constant travel, and threatening phone calls in the middle of the night.

Our marriage has been nurtured by the grace and intercession of Rev. Dr. Elliott Mason and others who love us, the insight of Bishop Walter Scott Thomas, a rededication ceremony by Rev. Dr. Samuel Proctor, a second honeymoon in Morocco, the confidence of Jamal and Thema, and the light in our granddaughters' eyes. These have combined to illumine our hope, ground us when overwhelmed, and in our darkest hour bring new light to help see us through.

Our marriage soars because of the power of the Holy Ghost, the favor of the Lord, the refuge of a home altar, our prophetic anointing, the grace to forgive, the humility to be changed, unceasing prayer, and the redeeming love of God. Our marriage has been molded in the image of God's love through the practice of spiritual disciplines wherein we pursue God's presence, God's direction, and God's heart. Some of these disciplines are shared in this volume.

The Sovereign LORD has given me an instructed tongue,
*   to know the word that sustains the weary.*
He wakens me morning by morning,
*   wakens my ear to listen like one being taught.*
*   —Isaiah 50:4 (NIV)*

A spiritual discipline is a unique system of devotions intended to build faith when consistently practiced over a period of time. For Christians desiring to grow in the love and knowledge of God, the disciplines are a gateway to intimacy and communion. By providing opportunities to revisit and reclaim the experiences and teachings of Jesus, the disciplines offer inroads to self-knowledge and spiritual power.

For the clergy spouse who lives in full public view, the pursuit of spiritual disciplines provides a much-needed opportunity for solitude. The disciplines quickly become a way to anchor our lives and help us establish healthy boundaries of personhood. They give us breathing room. A continuous, ongoing, faithful practice of spiritual disciplines can provide order, clarity, and confidence, especially in times of emotional upheaval.

Spiritual disciplines adhere to the precepts of Scripture, but are neither so rigid nor inflexible as to prohibit freedom of intuition, expression, and reflection. The disciplines require primarily an inward retreat from immediate circumstances. To be effective, those spiritual disciplines that require internal reflection thrive in separation, silence, and stillness. The mastery of the labyrinth of spiritual disciplines leads the practitioner home to his or her divine center of love awareness.

Once mastered, the disciplines move the practitioner from revelation to actualization. Indeed, the visions I have received from the Holy Spirit through the sustained practice of spiritual disciplines manifest themselves in every area of my life—relationships, living space, priorities—in ways that are identifiable and irrefutable. The divine and mundane are melded so as to keep the practitioner both lifted and grounded.

The disciplines are proved and approved! Before going forward, however, I must provide one caveat to the use of spiritual disciplines. The practices outlined in this volume are not intended to replace the intervention of mental health professionals. Feelings of embarrassment or shame should not prevent one from seeking professional mental health care. Indeed, the difficulties of covenant clergy marriage may be eased by such intervention.

The disciplines are both fallible and extraordinary. Faith, integrity, and consistency will greatly influence your results. Orthodoxy and improvisation in the disciplines create offerings that awaken, focus, illumine, stretch, and compel. Embrace the path that most clearly calls to you. Drink deeply of the healing of the Lord as you journey day by day. Remember, the quality of life that we live rests largely with the kinds of decisions we make. Surely God has given us both the power and the authority to live a beautiful life.

> *"LORD, you shine on my life like the sun;*
> *you protect me like a shield.*
> *You alone have blessed me with favor, honor,*
> *and every good thing." (see Psalm 84:11-12)*

The practice of spiritual disciplines has given roots and wings to my marriage and to my ministry. Through the guidance of the Holy Spirit, I have been privileged to share the art of spiritual disciplines with clergy spouses and others worldwide. Whether people are facing the challenges of divorce, poor self-esteem, or even death, the practice of spiritual disciplines has provided direction and kept its practitioners centered in the things of God while dealing with the journey through human relationships with spouses and those to whom they minister.

When a clergy spouse is angry, hurt, or confused, the last thing he or she wants to hear is another sermon or lecture. I have found that one of the most effective means of connecting with, and providing support, comfort, and advice to clergy spouses is through letter writing. Letters can be read and reread and recalled years later. They express ideas that are orally ineffective. Letter writing, uncommon in today's world of e-mailing and text messaging, is a sacred art. Indeed, much Scripture that undergirds and inspires us today takes the form of epistles, letters written to the early church. The paradox of writing and receiving letters is that it is a form of communication that provides both intimacy and distance.

The letters contained in this volume are not abstract reflections or philosophical teachings. The eyes and hearts of the spouses to whom they were first written are known to me. Each letter is a composite representation written to those who have had similar concerns, struggles, or issues. I have diluted, camouflaged, and consolidated facts in order to protect the identity of these companions on the journey.

It is my prayer that this experience will have the practical effect of making the journey through covenant clergy marriage less burdensome. But more than that, I pray that God's light will shine more brightly in the lives of those who seek to embrace it.

Before beginning the spiritual disciplines, I suggest that you recruit two or three personal intercessors—they can be fellow clergy spouses—for the journey into the light. The conspiracy of silence cripples the healing process for many clergy marriages. We are not alone. We are never alone! As you begin this journey, ask the Lord to reveal to you the person or persons who will pray for you in confidentiality, purity, and compassion.

God once said, "Let the light shine out of darkness!" This is the same God who made his light shine in our hearts by letting us know the glory of God that is in the face of Christ.

LETTER 1

Keturah

Self-esteem

How glorious is the name of the Lord!
How immeasurable the compassion flowing
from the womb of the divine.
Tomorrow holds her breath.
Yesterday vanishes with each rising of the sun.
But today is the perfect host of our confidence and joy.

Dear Keturah,

At the dedication ceremony for the new headquarters of the
National Council of Negro Women, President Emerita Dr.
Dorothy Height proclaimed, "We are more than we think we
are!" Whether conceived in pain or bliss, these are healing words
for African American women of every generation. Whether our
journey has been flooded with affirmation or wrought with sorrow, whether all our dreams have come true or we remain hostage
to our darkest nightmare, "we are more than we think we are!"

With that in mind, there is no healthy or holy reason for marriage to diminish your self-esteem. Before the throne of God we all
stand both inadequate and forgiven. Despite that, in the moment
when you feel unworthy, consider that to God you are "a little
lower than the angels" (Psalm 8:5, NKJV). You must embrace your
standing in God's realm unconditionally. To be a symbolic or rit-
ualistic first lady is bogus. Being an authentic spouse requires an

affirmation within your soul that embraces all that God has made you. Our husbands cannot give us identity; only God can. Our spouses can only share with us their own souls' longing for completion. Consider the words of the poet William Waring Cuney: "She does not know her own beauty." Do not let these words be your epithet. Rather, say of the life of challenge and opportunity before you, "I was born for this!"

Part of what contributes to our feelings of inadequacy as clergy spouses is a basic misunderstanding of the nature of marriage. We tend to believe marriage occurs once-and-for-all at an altar. But in truth, we marry daily. The covenant is renewed with each break of day. With each slice of toast, with each song of the morning, with each disaster of communication, with each tender glance, with each bill that must remain unpaid, with each overlooked fault, with each interfering relative, with each too-long church meeting, we marry daily. Each time, the breadth of the covenant grows more luminous. As it grows, so, too, do our feelings that we are in a place of overwhelming, unwieldy transformation.

And so, we get tired. And when we feel exhausted, we assume that our marriage is exhausted. Your marriage may not be exhausted; you are. Your task is to work with your spouse through the power of the Holy Spirit to make the journey toward covenant clergy union one of fulfillment. To do so, I recommend the following course of action.

Know Yourself

A woman who is prepared to walk the path of covenant relationship already knows who she is. Don't buy into the first lady hype. A symbol cannot breathe; it cannot give life. Your husband cannot make you whole. He can hold your hand when you find yourself walking through the valley and cheer you on as you climb the mountains of your own prophetic potential. But you must know yourself for yourself. Not just your address and your dress size.

But what causes you to take a second look? What word can you hear over and over again and it would never be too much? When does starlight catch you smiling? Is there a song in you that wants to sing? A tear agonizing to be shed? A dream tucked away in forgetfulness?

Know your own thoughts about the state of the world, about stem cell research, about the death penalty, about the elimination of poverty, about the future, and about the kingdom of God! Know the meaning of your own truth about the Incarnation, Crucifixion, and Resurrection; miracles and mysteries; good and evil; providence and volition; beauty, death, and change.

Know your sorrow—acknowledge it, respect it, release it.

Know your weaknesses—do not rationalize or justify them. Keep them in a place where they can be transformed. Never advertise or flaunt them. Apologize quickly when others are affected by them.

Know your strengths. You have many: personality, cultural, emotional, organizational, relational, domestic, financial, and personal sense of style.

Your self-worth can never be measured simply in terms of the tangible, visible, material criteria of the culture. Cultural cues sometimes debase our self-worth. If you are having difficulty determining what makes you "more than you think you are," just think about what you would say and do for a little five-year-old girl weighed down with insecurity and low self-esteem. Write it down. Then begin to say and do those things for yourself daily.

Loving yourself does not require perfection, but compassion. Self-love should not be postponed until the perfect comes. It is nurtured by gratitude and humility. When we are alone, self-love allows us to relax. When we are with others, self-love allows us to be confident and unimposing. A woman with healthy self-love is a magnet for success, friendship, and creative expression. She is thoughtful. She is a visionary. She is self-aware without being self-conscious. She is radiant with the glory that Jesus has given her.

Whoever pursues godliness and unfailing love will find life, godliness, and honor. (Proverbs 21:21, NLT)

Knowing yourself will give you the peace of mind and confidence to assume your important role in a covenant clergy marriage. Knowing yourself is a never-ending process, one that you will visit and revisit. Yet you must also gain confidence in other tasks that will lead to a fulfilled relationship.

Take Time for Love

You and your spouse need to take time for love. If you don't have love, you don't have anything. Love is all there is. Board meetings, conferences, and community expectations will pass away. God has planted you at the spacious center of divine love. There is glory all around you. The morning star will shine in your sky. Soak it up. It will not consume you. Take time to illuminate in the afterglow of passion.

Allow your sensuality to be liberated. You should feel comfortable discussing your intimacy needs and experiences with your husband. Neither of you should experience discomfort, pain, or inadequacy within your intimate union. Reading passages to each other from the Song of Solomon is powerful foreplay and makes for great long-distance loving when the telephone is your only connection.

Be mindful that intimacy, although it very much includes sexual love and affection, is much greater than these alone. At its height, intimacy can be a wordless union of souls that ignites a glow within us that can be sustained only by the spirit of the Lord.

Establish the Home as Sacred Space

Whoever coined the phrase "home, sweet home" expressed for all time and all people the bliss of personal sanctuary. We can never feel as safe, as loved, or as violated or betrayed as we can at home. Be it ever so humble, "There's no place like home." Like Dorothy, we go home to escape Oz, the fantasy forced upon us by circumstances. Any spouse who attempts to create a life or sustain a marriage while living in a fantasy world will be brutally brought down. Home can be shaped into sacred space using creativity, passion, and humor. The following ground rules will assist you to make your home a sacred space:

- No church files, papers, or meetings in the home
- No church phone calls during meals
- No staff presence during personal time
- No conflict on Saturdays (the day before Sunday service)

"My house shall be called
a house of prayer . . ." Matthew 21:13 (NRSV)

As it is with the congregation, so it is with the disciple. We are to abide in prayer. Let prayer be your dwelling place, your residence, your center, your mansion, your palace.

Too often we neglect the home as a sanctuary for prayer. Prayer is a very special way to create intimacy within marriage. Praying together is a wonderful place for any couple with a shared desire for blessings to awaken a fresh sense of oneness, wholeness, and union. I would despair to think whether my own marriage of almost forty years could have endured even the first five years had it not been for prayer. Whether silent or audible, prayer is effective and essential. To pray while lying in each other's arms is glorious. The spirit of the Lord will complete your coming together.

"For where two or three are gathered in my name, I am
there among them." (Matthew 18:20, NRSV)

We live many years with broken hearts. The trauma is magnified when the one to whom you have given your life demonstrates neither awareness nor compassion regarding your pain. He is the source of your frustration as well as your affirmation and applause. And, yes, it is hurtful to watch so many others—the church, the public, the denomination—honor and celebrate him so profusely that he is insulated from constructive criticism. But prayer can create the setting for you to articulate your pain and for you to hear his. Some anxiety, stress, or depression is a reality of life for those in leadership or public life.

When you have a history of depression or are experiencing a prolonged state of anxiety, it is urgent that, in addition to prayer, you seek the help of a Christian mental health licensed professional. Do not allow bad theology or shame to prevent you from tapping into a valuable resource.

You have the power to decide that you will never become your husband's cross to bear. Affirm within your soul that you "may prosper and be in good health" (3 John 1:2, NASB). Covenant clergy marriages must be intentional about emotional wellness. To have access to "every spiritual blessing in the heavenly places" (Ephesians 1:3, NKJV) and remain in a perpetual state of dysfunction is unnecessary and immature. Intend to live a life radiant with confidence, enthusiasm, and grace. You are much "more than you think you are," to your husband and to the kingdom of God. Begin to pursue your destiny in bold and flaming strides toward your prophetic purpose. Get excited about what is being born in you.

There is another reason your home needs to be healing ground. Husband and wife must know that there is a place where fidelity, confidentiality, vulnerability, and weaknesses may safely enter the healing process. This place must be home. Home is your altar, your refreshment, your place of rest, beauty, and dreaming. Home is your garden of memories, the tabernacle of your passion, the playground for your laughter. The meaning of home can never be bought, erased, or lost. It remains with us, although sometimes hidden in the pockets of our sorrow. Home provides the lens through which we view the whole world. Wherever we are, home is never far from us. For your soul's sake, keep home holy, healthy, and happy.

Although we are in a constant struggle to keep the spirit of materialism in restraint, it continues to surface in ways that violate the authentic meaning of "home." Appliances, furnishings, "curb appeal," accessories, and the like, if not recognized as mere things, can become little altars of idolatry. The value of a home has everything to do with the quality of life and relationship of those who dwell therein and nothing to do with the price tag.

"... but as for me and my household, we will serve the LORD." Joshua 24:15 (NRSV)

Rejoice in the integrity of your faith.
Delight in the sincerity of your compassion.
Honor the grace with which you serve.
Celebrate the hours, the days, the years of your devotion.
Commemorate every courageous act.
Shine in the glory of your own personhood.
Shine without hesitation or doubt.
Shine with the face of a newborn.
Shine from within.
Shine.

◆

I pray also that the eyes of your heart may be enlightened in order that you may know the hope to which he has called you, the riches of his glorious inheritance in the saints, and his incomparably great power for us who believe. (Ephesians 1:18-19, NIV)

Lectio Divina

The spiritual discipline that I recommend to you, Keturah, is that of *lectio divina*, an ancient art practiced widely by Christians. *Lectio divina* is a slow, contemplative praying of the Scriptures that enables the Word of God to become a means of union with God. The Word of God is spirit and life. As you prepare to approach the Word of God, anticipate God's presence. Release all pre-existing interpretations of your chosen passage. Be open to a fresh and new experience. How much you read does not matter. Rather, how well the Spirit of the Word penetrates your life and how deeply you imbibe God's Spirit is of importance.

Begin the practice by sitting with your Bible in a quiet place. Quietness will allow you to fully emerge in the authenticity of your humanity and hear your own thoughts. Become familiar with the energy that silence brings. Teach yourself how to embrace it. Do nothing. Simply be present to life.

Once you have practiced silence, any one of the following affirmations will assist you as you begin to pray the Scriptures:

"My desire to listen to the heart of God shall be undistracted."

"The presence of the Lord brings healing to my life."

"My prophetic purpose is established by communion with the Lord."

When you internalize these affirmations, your thoughts about yourself will receive fresh manna. Once you are at home with silence and have allowed the affirmations to shape the pattern of your thinking, you are ready to practice the discipline.

As you locate the text that will be the focus of today's journey, thank God for the light that you are about to receive. If you are challenged with finding a passage with which to begin, I recommend Psalm 139. Slowly begin to read-pray the passage, not more than five to seven verses at time. Honor each word. If you are compelled, reread the same word, sentence, or passage.

These suggestions will help you make the most of this experience:

• Take your time.
• Be open to the heart of God. Do not bring your agenda to the Scripture.
• Engage all of your senses as you pray.
• Listen intently for God's voice (but do not be alarmed if revelations are slow in coming) to impart wisdom, counsel, consolation, and new energy for living.
• End each session with a familiar prayer or song.

As the path empowers you to bridge the gap in your self-worth, you will be able to come to terms with the impact your former self has had on your marital relationship. As you begin to take an inventory of the changes you are making in your perception, communication, and spiritual understanding, become the renaissance wife in your worship, prayer life, lovemaking, and public and private presence. Let your home and friendships be aglow with generosity of spirit. As you touch the heart of

God, you will feel yourself soaring within. If you are devoted to spiritual practice, you will begin to traverse horizons of revelation unknown to people who limit their encounter with God to Sunday morning liturgy.

Insecurity is a hindering spirit whose only purpose is to keep the people of God locked behind the unreality of intimidation. Once you step out and stand up for your divine purpose, the enemy is silenced. You have the power to live beyond self-rejection and self-criticism and silence the emotional slander perpetrated by low self-esteem. The light in you is light, indeed. "Therefore let us cast off the works of darkness, and let us put on the armor of light" (Romans 13:12, NKJV). It's time for you to fight back. Take your power back, and let the light of heaven shine through you!

Change

Do not conform any longer to the pattern of this world,
but be transformed by the renewing of your mind.
(Romans 12:2, NIV)

Dear Zipporah,

Love changes us in subtle yet profound ways. Love's energies bring new vocabulary, different priorities, and, for some of us, a change of style. We are not always aware of the many ways that loving and being loved transforms who we are. Those who are flexible, intuitive, and have an open personality seem to adapt well even to extensive change.

For the covenant clergy marriage, change is a fact of life. When you enter the life of a clergy spouse, you change from being a private person to becoming a public figure whose time is rarely yours to do with as you please. You are a servant to the liturgical calendar who quickly learns that the Lord's Day is Sunday and any other day that necessity raises its head.

At some time or many times in your marriage, a geographical change may be required. Moving to another city, state, or country can prove challenging. Quite often, the family is forced into unknown territory, leaving trusted friends and a familiar and comfortable culture behind. As clergy spouses, we often struggle with change, especially those over which we have no control.

Unfortunately, you did not embrace change gracefully. Being uprooted made you hostile. You went to the new church with a chip on your shoulder. Your anger was directed at people whom you did not know and who had done nothing to you. Now that you have had time to calm down, you feel ashamed. Having pushed away those who tried to welcome you, you feel isolated. Now you are a soul living under conviction for being verbally abusive and petty. You want to know how you can make a comeback after all you have done. Remember that "with God all things are possible" (Matthew 19:26, NIV).

I applaud the integrity you demonstrated by owning your role in the mess. It would be easy to blame the denomination, your husband, or both. I also applaud your husband, who has chosen to love you in spite of yourself. Now, you must choose to love yourself enough to expose the many layers of self-deception that are operating in your life. This will take hard work on your part. Don't get discouraged along the way as you attempt to make the changes and pursue the path that will release your magnificence. This journey takes patience. Be patient with yourself, your husband, and God.

Before beginning to live a new way, you must first be forgiven of your past. Ask for God's forgiveness for your failure to represent God well. Then ask for your husband's forgiveness. Your husband has paid the price for your rage. It has cost him emotionally and administratively. Yet, his love for you has cushioned your marriage. During this time, allow God's love and your husband's love to embrace and sustain you. Also, if there are specific individuals whom you have offended, ask their forgiveness. Most difficult, but perhaps most important, forgive yourself. You must never let past failures limit your destiny.

Because of what you have been through, your mind, heart, and will are open to the possibility of change. This is your season of change. Do not let it pass. I suggest you begin with the discipline of divine intention. An intention is a clear and present purpose directive of the soul. Through intention, you can be ushered into a God-breathed life. The work of divine intention is to equip the practitioner to master her own will.

The will, like a roaring lion refusing to be domesticated, resists any attempt to bring the ego into submission. But unless the will is subject to the Holy Spirit, there can be no change. The power you receive through mastery of your will can change the way the world sees you and the way you see and understand yourself. Restoration will come to you by the grace of God.

Divine intention is a countercultural journey that rejects materialism, competition, and compulsive gratification. Its practitioner pursues only those qualities that draw eternity. More than any of these things, divine intention consecrates life to the glory of God. Hold fast to your divine intentions, and you will heal your life.

The Beatitudes as a Foundation for the Practice of Divine Intention

The foundation for divine intention is found in Matthew 5:1-12:

When Jesus saw the crowds, he went up the mountain; and after he sat down, his disciples came to him. Then he began to speak, and taught them, saying:

"Blessed are the poor in spirit, for theirs is the kingdom of heaven.

"Blessed are those who mourn, for they will be comforted.

"Blessed are the meek, for they will inherit the earth.

"Blessed are those who hunger and thirst for righteousness, for they will be filled.

"Blessed are the merciful, for they will receive mercy.

"Blessed are the pure in heart, for they will see God.

"Blessed are the peacemakers, for they will be called children of God.

"Blessed are those who are persecuted for righteousness' sake, for theirs is the kingdom of heaven.

"Blessed are you when people revile you and persecute you and utter all kinds of evil against you falsely on my account. Rejoice and be glad, for your reward is great in heaven, for in the same way they persecuted the prophets who were before you." (NRSV)

The Beatitudes summon us to an authentic relationship with God while opening our hearts and lives to others. For that reason, I am recommending that they serve as the basis of your spiritual discipline. The Beatitudes encompass three universal intentions that can transform consciousness, thereby transforming life.

Be holy. In all things, strive to be as God is. Be led by the Spirit of the Lord rather than emotion or opinion. Live God. Be God's authentic presence on the earth. Let your heart be in continuous worship.

Be compassionate. Be the peace. Unleash your power to heal. Forgive always. Love all. Exemplify God's generosity.

Be harmless. See the good and acknowledge it. Win souls for Jesus. Renounce all violence of thought, word, and deed. Be captive to grace. Put others first.

Only a soul fully endued with the mind of Christ and love of Calvary can pursue the beatific intentions. They require supernatural momentum and absolute humility. When God finds us in the place of brokenness, the desire to be whole outdistances any other aspiration, such as wealth, comfort, or recognition.

By these intentions, the human soul resonates with the breath of God, making time on the planet fluorescent with love. You will not desire to waver from the path of God. You will see, hear, and know the movement of God in the earth. Purged of every corrupting impulse, the heart of God shines all the more. Be holy. Be compassionate. Be harmless. You must embrace them all together.

The Practice of Divine Intention

Behavioral science teaches us that it takes twenty-one days to develop a habit. Therefore, I challenge you to vow to devote the next twenty-one days to a life shaped and informed by the three beatific intentions. From the moment you awaken, recite, reflect, and be refreshed by each intention. Dedicate five minutes seven times a day to meditating on the intentions. Let each intention speak to you, counsel you, and chastise you. Know that an inward change must precede every other!

From the moment you embrace the intentions, you will begin to experience yourself as holy, compassionate, and harmless. Keep your Bible near so that you can research passages of Scripture on holiness, compassion, and harmlessness. Memorize those passages that speak to you. Allow them to breathe into your life. Also make note of situations and personalities you find difficult to process. Let these challenging circumstances and people become your prayer intentions.

As you engage in this practice, your intentions will become the desires of your heart. Knowing that if you trust God, God will give you what you desire, you can declare boldly: I am holy; I am compassionate; I am harmless. Yes, an intention that begins as a prayer and is internalized as a purpose will eventually manifest as a lifestyle value. It is a collaboration of heart, soul, and will under the guidance of the Holy Spirit.

> *Oh, what joy for those*
> *whose rebellion is forgiven,*
> *whose sin is put out of sight!*
> *Yes, what joy for those*
> *whose record the LORD has cleared of sin,*
> *whose lives are lived in complete honesty!*
> *—Psalm 32:1-2 (NLT)*

At the end of this letter, you will find a daily framework for the practice of divine intentions. Use it as the Holy Spirit guides, knowing that neither the intentions nor the practice thereof is meant to bind you. Their work is to open the gates of freedom to your destiny, to offer you a fresh understanding of life, marriage, and ministry. The more you internalize the core intentions, the less likely you will be to slide back into a negative personality rut and the more likely you are to bring light into the world.

Slowly You Will Grow

Our lives are a reflection of the decisions that we have made over time. Decisions have created habits, values, psychological responses, and perceptions. The challenge to divine intention is to dismantle our decision-making infrastructure as we learn to make new decisions. Godly decisions must become our daily bread without exception or exemption. There will be times when you may show residue of your former self. At times the path will seem unclear to you. Wait for a sign. There is sure to be one. Do not be misled by false prophets, deceivers, and perpetrators along the way. Know that good Samaritans, wise men, and shepherds will meet you on your journey. The adventure you are about to undertake will also have a great impact on those you encounter on your path to wholeness. Be motivated by the magnificence that awaits you. Know that you have available to you the tools that make lasting change possible. Remember that God is with you.

> Do not fear, for I am with you,
>   do not be afraid, for I am your God;
> I will strengthen you, I will help you,
>   I will uphold you with my victorious right hand.
> —Isaiah 41:10 (NRSV)

The miracle of divine intention lies as much in the process as in the results. The next twenty-one days are crucial, but they are only the beginning. You may not be able to grasp the long-term impact of your journey at first. But in time, God's transforming power will become manifest.

The beatific intentions will produce miraculous results in your marriage. Indeed, beatific intentions in marriage have a way of making marital bliss tangible. The ministry will also begin to flourish in new ways. You will gain a sense of presence that is deeper than what you wear. Your stream of influence will undergo a positive expansion. Your husband's heart will hold you in honor, and the wounds inflicted upon your marriage will begin to heal as the marriage is transformed.

How will you know when your change has come? When living the beatific intentions becomes effortless; when your desire to commune with God is greater than your need for anything else; when you are excited about reading the Word of God; when praying for others brings you joy; when your husband's vision for ministry becomes your hope in God; when you know your own magnificence; when light is drawn to you; when you can laugh at yourself; when you can walk compassionately alongside another woman who feels the need to change her life, then you will know that you have been changed!

How will you know when you have become one who embodies holiness, compassion, and harmlessness? When you have reached the state where only God matters. Your desire is only God. Your life's motivation is only God. When, after you have spoken, passed by, or your name is mentioned, all that is said is, "Only God," your intentions have been realized!

So, my beloved sister, make your intentions known. Paint them in broad strokes. Wear them like a banner around your heart. Make of them the lyrics to your new soul melody. Pour them like new wine into the cup of your marriage. They can be the cement that holds your life together, a mirror of God's favor, the summit of your aspirations and the manna that feeds you in the wilderness. Be holy. Be compassionate. Be harmless. And your light will truly shine.

Eye has not seen, nor ear heard,
Nor have entered into the heart of [woman]
The things which God has prepared for those
* who love Him.*
—1 Corinthians 2:9 (NKJV)

Twenty-one Days—A Journey of Beatific Intention

You will need a Bible and a journal that you can keep with you throughout the day. Be sensitive to any spiritual promptings; whether an image, a thought, or a word.

BE HOLY.
BE COMPASSIONATE.
BE HARMLESS.

It would be lacking in humility to advertise that you are in this process.

Allow your soul, imagination, and behavior to be held captive by the Scriptures indicated.

Days 1–7: The Purging

Yes, we must "detox" our inner life. During the course of an ordinary 24-hour period we take in many impurities. The environment, the culture, the brokenness of humanity—all harbor contagious strains of sin, unbelief, and rebellion, so let each of us purify our souls "through the word of the living and enduring God" (1 Peter 1:22 *note*, NRSV).

From rising until noon: Holiness

For five minutes, acknowledge, recite, and embrace the holiness within you (Matthew 5:3).

From noon until 6:00 p.m.: Compassion

For five to seven minutes, focus upon, recite, and demonstrate the compassion within you (Matthew 5:7).

From 6:00 p.m. until bedtime: Harmlessness

For five to ten minutes, meditate upon and breathe the harmlessness within you (Matthew 5:11-12).

Days 9–14: The Unfolding of the Trinity

The highest aim of humanity is to know God. Be open to a fresh experience with the Lord. Discard your familiar crutches and let the eyes of your heart be opened. "I AM" speaks. "For they shall all know me, from the least of them to the greatest, says the LORD" (Jeremiah 31:34, NKJV).

From rising until noon: Holiness

Know yourself as the image of God. Internalize your intention: "I am a vessel of the righteousness of God" (see Matthew 5:6).

From noon until 6:00 p.m.: Compassion

Reflect upon the sonship of Jesus. Manifest your intention: "I am peace" (see Matthew 5:9).

From 6:00 p.m. until bedtime: Harmlesness

Abide in the Holy Spirit. Breathe your intention: "My thoughts shine with the light of God" (see Matthew 5:8).

Days 15–21: Manifestation

"All things came into being through him" (John 1:3, NRSV). When we spend time with God, it is evident to believers and unbelievers. There will be an intangible shining over your life, an inner glow, a freedom, a magnificent grace. As in the case of Zechariah, ". . . and they realized that he had seen a vision . . ." (Luke 1:22, NRSV).

From rising until noon: Holiness

Fast if permitted by your physician. Seek total union with God in prayer and Scripture (Psalm 95:6).

From noon until 6:00 p.m.: Compassion

Live as an oblation (a love offering). Bless all with whom you interact (Matthew 16:19).

From 6:00 p.m. until bedtime: Harmlessness

Forgive all. Release all. Love all (1 John 4:7).

As you continue the journey, expand the breadth of your intentions. Enlarge the scope of your world view. Penetrate the boundaries you have set for your life. Seize every opportunity to experience and bless the nations. Confront and dismantle all resistance. Embrace your status among the community of the faithful as you give birth to intentions that will have cosmic impact.

You are holy.
You are compassionate.
You are harmless.

Give yourself permission to begin your twenty-one days over again and again and again and again until you are free to confess: "I am . . ."

Bethesda

Church Conflict

For when we came into Macedonia, this body
of ours had no rest, but we were harassed at
every turn—conflicts on the outside, fears within.
(2 Corinthians 7:5, NIV)

Precious Bethesda,

May the peace and grace of our Lord Jesus Christ flood your heart
with the healing light of God's presence.

A church in turmoil is nothing new. Indeed, the epistles in Scripture are inspired responses to conflict among the people of God.
Even before God became flesh among us, the children of Israel
had their share of conflict. And so it is today. Wherever two or
three are gathered, the existence of conflict is inevitable. But,
thanks be to God, God is inevitably in the midst. God's healing
light can shine in spite of the turmoil.

I know of nothing more devastating for a clergy spouse than for
the pastor to be at the center of a church conflict. Not even the
death of a spouse has the potential to create longer-lasting soul
trauma. Church conflicts can place you and your family at ground
zero emotionally, psychologically, and spiritually. Church conflict
is especially troubling to children who, in their formative years,
are exposed to the underside of the faith. It can affect their perception of the church and of God for years to come.

But fear not, you can emerge from this season battered, perhaps, but not permanently scarred. You can become a woman centered by prevailing prayer and a powerful sense of self who has made great strides toward her divine destiny. No doubt you will be affected by what is happening between your husband and members of the church, but you can avoid being dominated by it. Pray the Holy Spirit to grant you the inner resilience of one who cannot be drawn into public or personality conflicts or moved by pettiness. Pray to be a woman of such mature faith who can worship without distraction and who, no matter what, absolutely trusts the love of God.

Do not repay anyone evil for evil. Be careful to do what is right in the eyes of everybody. If it is possible, as far as depends on you, live at peace with everyone. (Romans 12:17-18, NIV)

Conflict in a church is never pleasant or simple. Moreover, the wife of a pastor embroiled in conflict can become both a buffer and a target. Those who lack substantive issues for grievance will take their focus off the budget, the mission, or the leadership priorities and concern themselves with demeaning the spouse. Your hairstyle, body type, parenting style, education, class, background, speech, friendships, birth family, and where you shop will become the object of their contempt. You may be subjected to innuendo, anonymous calls, unsigned letters, rumors, or even blurts of sarcasm as you pass. If they cannot win the victory, they will be satisfied with stealing your joy.

Church conflict has the potential to destroy your church, your husband, and you. This is why you must stay attuned to the light and not depart from it. Only God knows the end from the beginning. If you become disconnected from the God of light, the power you need to manage the conflict will soon be depleted.

As much as you may be plagued by an aching sense of powerlessness, avoid falling prey to a victim role. Yet, in your effort not to be victimized, do not become vengeful. Remember, the best revenge against those who persecute you is to have a beautiful life. Decide that the battle will not destroy you. Do not give anyone or anything the power to diminish your joy in the service of the Lord or the beauty of your marriage.

"For this reason, since the day we heard it, we have not ceased praying for you and asking that you may be filled with the knowledge of God's will in all spiritual wisdom and understanding." (Colossians 1:9, NRSV)

Your Role in Church Conflict

You should recognize two things about your role in church conflict. First and foremost, as a clergy spouse, you have no authority or legitimacy in a church fight. So you must publicly stay out of it. The best you can do is to pray with and encourage your husband. Second, church conflict is not brought to closure by any one set of rules or patterns. There are, however, a few strategies of engagement you might offer your husband privately:

1. Determine the real source of the conflict and focus on diffusing it. At times, the issue people appear to be fighting is not what they are really fighting about. Remember that fear is usually an underlying source of conflict—fear of change, fear of growth, fear of displacement.
2. Recruit supportive friends and clergy associates to pray for your family and ministry. Seek the counsel of a seasoned pastor you trust.
3. Take mental health breaks by going to couples' retreats, cultural or sporting events, or other family outings.
4. Enlist the assistance of a mediator. Mediation is a process by which pastor and aggrieved members engage a mutually agreed upon third party to help bring closure to the conflict and reconciliation between the parties involved.
5. Find fortitude through fasting. Consistently fasting as a couple once or twice weekly will rearrange your outward priorities and restore your soul. Any fast should be taken with the approval of your physician. By fasting you will gain a kingdom perspective and inner resilience.

Managing Church Conflict

The LORD *will keep you from all evil;*
he will keep your life.
The LORD *will keep*
your going out and your coming in
from this time on and forever more.
—*Psalm 121:7-8 (NRSV)*

Once you understand your role in the conflict, you can focus your energy on providing a healthy environment through which you and your family can navigate the sometimes treacherous terrain. This will require of you a renewed mind. A renewed mind can develop in your husband and you a confident and loving demeanor that will help your children better process the remnants of the conflict, such as rumors passed on by their peers. Let your children know that they are safe and loved and that you and your husband are not worried. Show them through Scripture God's promises to protect your family.

Most of all, when you develop the appropriate strategies for coping with church conflict, your children are bound to follow your example. Therefore, just as the airlines instruct passengers traveling with small children to put their oxygen masks on before placing one on the child, you must lead your children to the light by first seeking the light yourself. I recommend that you adopt the following practice to help keep your marriage fresh and your family positive in the midst of conflict:

1. Hallow the name of Jesus whenever you begin to feel anxious.
2. Express God's love even if you are provoked.
3. Anticipate joy!
4. Let yourself rest often.
5. Envision the hand of God holding you up.
6. Nourish the good.
7. Practice gratitude.

Therefore take up the whole armor of God, so that you may be able to withstand on that evil day, and having done everything, to stand firm. Stand therefore, and fasten the belt of truth around your waist, and put on the breastplate of righteousness. As shoes for your feet put on whatever will make you ready to proclaim the gospel of peace. With all of these, take the shield of faith, with which you will be able to quench all the flaming arrows of the evil one. Take the helmet of salvation, and the sword of the Spirit, which is the word of God. (Ephesians 6:13-17, NRSV)

The seven practices will keep your thoughts from being held hostage to fear, bitterness, revenge, or doubt. If you are a person who has medically diagnosed depression, be sure to share this additional stress with your mental health care provider. This will allow him or her to monitor its effect on your mental well-being.

"Blessed are those who are persecuted for righteousness' sake, for theirs is the kingdom of heaven.

"Blessed are you when people revile you and persecute you and utter all kinds of evil against you falsely on my account. Rejoice and be glad, for your reward is great in heaven, for in the same way they persecuted the prophets who were before you." (Matthew 5:10-12, NRSV)

Embracing the Sabbath

Perhaps the most important practice in which you can engage as a clergy family, especially one embattled in conflict, is to create a sabbath atmosphere in your home.

We are commanded to "remember the sabbath day, to keep it holy" (Exodus 20:8, KJV). How easily we forget this charge, especially in clergy families. Usually, Sunday is not a day of rest for us. In fact, it is the most demanding and exhausting day of the week. Conflict causes added stress to the holy day. I recommend, therefore, that your home become your place of rest and that you use sabbath keeping as your path to inner light.

◆

Remember the resting of the Lord. The ethos of your home can be sacramental. Upon entering, one's soul will be embraced by the shalom of God. An extraordinary peace. A lifting of the heaviness of circumstances. Supreme acceptance. Flooded by the light. Agape. A place where every day is a day of grace. The place where revelation, laughter, rest, communication, and feasting are without interruption. And there is no fear. Most of all, there is no fear. Your home is the dwelling place of God's Spirit. Holy ground. A sanctuary.

Creating a Sabbath Home

Whether after a long journey, a tedious day, or a troubling experience, the two words that have the greatest power to heal are "Welcome home."

"God gives the desolate a home to live in," declares Psalm 68:6 (NRSV).

Home is a sacred gift, "be it ever so humble." It is a divine opportunity, a fountain of grace, your place of rest.

- Reclaim your home for sabbath room by room. Let light, beauty, natural foods, and scents that are calming (lavender), energizing (citrus), meditative (sandalwood), or sensual (jasmine) pervade your home. Let the atmosphere be welcoming.
- Adorn your space with symbols of life, such as plants, water features, fresh flowers, and artwork that projects peace and healing.
- Free your bedroom from the presence of energy-draining documents such as bills, reports, and files. Let your bedroom become an exclusive domain where you and your husband minister to each other.
- Set aside time daily for family prayer and Scripture reading.

- Set aside time for family meetings to process the church conflict and the disagreements among you.
- Allow the healing sounds of music to fill the atmosphere.
- Light a candle as you pray prayers of thanksgiving at the close of each day.
- Because our experiences outside the home have an impact on family life, choose wisely the kinds of people and situations that you expose yourselves to. Remember, there *are* still wonderful Christians who are not caught up in gossip, blogging, pettiness, or inciting rumors.
- Take advantage of women's retreats, prayer groups, and Bible studies.
- Allow your children to be guests at Sunday school or vacation Bible school at neighboring churches. This will allow them to grow spiritually without the pressure of being the preacher's kids, as well as providing an opportunity to meet new Christian friends.

"When you go through deep waters and great trouble, I will be with you. When you go through rivers of difficulty, you will not drown! When you walk through the fire of oppression, you will not be burned up; the flames will not consume you. For I am the LORD, your God, the Holy One of Israel, your Savior." (Isaiah 43:2-3, NLT)

The Solace of the Psalms

Even after conflict dies down or ceases, your need for sabbath will not diminish. For we were not made for the sabbath, but the sabbath was made for us (see Mark 2:27). Sabbath keeping must, therefore, become a permanent part of your family life. As you strive to maintain a perpetual sabbath in your home, I recommend you drink deeply of the consolation found in the psalms. The psalms can be used to teach your children compassion and forgiveness. I especially recommend that you adopt Psalm 91 as your mantra, even as a lifestyle. The following verses of Psalm 91 (NIV) you may find particularly useful:

I will say of the LORD, "He is my refuge and my fortress, my God, in whom I trust." (v. 2)

He will cover you with his feathers, and under his wings you will find refuge; his faithfulness will be your shield and rampart. (v. 4)

You will not fear the terror of night, nor the arrow that flies by day. (v. 5)

For he will command his angels concerning you to guard you in all your ways. (v. 11)

"Because he loves me," says the LORD, "I will rescue him; I will protect him, for he acknowledges my name." (v. 14)

"He will call upon me, and I will answer him; I will be with him in trouble, I will deliver him and honor him." (v. 15)

Your home is the perfect context for developing and shaping a Psalm 91 way of life. Psalm 91 will allow you to embrace a life without excess, one that is free from clutter and disorder, where the volume is turned down on criticism and turned up on praise, a life of shared responsibility, where there is always time for fun and love.

Set aside sixteen one-hour segments over the next month. Commit to reading Psalm 91, focusing on one verse each segment. Give yourself completely to its meaning and power. You will be amazed by the dynamic influence upon your faith formation. When your expectation is that God will provide rest at a time when your ministry is embroiled in controversy, your livelihood at risk, and your reputation vulnerable, you will have entered a place of abiding grace, a place unthinkable for unbelievers and superstitious to the cynical. Hour by hour, drink the sweet milk of Psalm 91 until you are fully attuned to the love of God.

It is not possible to hold anxiety-provoking thoughts and thoughts of rest at the same time. One mindset will have to surrender to the other. You must envision what may seem impossible except by faith. See your marriage resting in the presence of the Lord. See it flourishing on prayer and altogether blessed in hope. See your marriage as having a promised future that includes good (see Jeremiah 29:11).

Let the new woman rise! She will throw off all vanity-emptiness. She will stand before the gates of her prophetic purpose. She will be the light in her household. She will rejoice in the unction of the Lord. She will fear no evil. When undergoing trials, she will invoke patience. She will put on her beautiful garments and not the apparel of defeat. She will shine! She will shine! She will shine!

You Are Not Alone

Many covenant clergy marriages have withstood the unthinkable: being locked out, sued, voted out, vandalized, rejected, homeless, and scandalized. They have survived schism, financial boycott, cross burning, interference, infiltration, instigation, rumor, riot, zealots, harlots, setbacks, standoffs, vision killers, character assassin, a holocaust of disinformation, and more. You are well able to endure and triumph whatever lies ahead. You are a spirit warrior, devoted, dedicated, and determined.

As a servant leader, you will always be engaged in some level of conflict. While I cannot tell you that everything will work out just the way you want, I can promise you that God will be with you. And God will give you rest, for "the Son of Man is Lord even of the Sabbath" (Mark 2:28, NIV).

Discouragement

"I have this complaint against you.
You don't love me or each other as you did at first!"
(Revelation 2:4, NLT)

Oh, Zion,

Several years ago, you were fired up and ready to go for Jesus. Since then, you have seen the naked church and are repulsed by the politics of carnality, the raw ambition, and the vanity therein! Halos have fallen from those you sought to emulate, and you have found that would-be mentors function more like control freaks. How can this be a foretaste of glory divine? If this is the church, "I may as well have stayed in the world," you may say to yourself.

I know this rude awakening is very difficult for you and your spouse. What your eyes have seen and your heart has felt is undeniable; however, you have drawn an erroneous conclusion. The self-centeredness of Peter and the cynicism of Thomas do not mitigate against the redeeming love of Jesus Christ; they make it necessary. The same is true for the Peters and Thomases of today.

You may be wondering how to get off this slippery slope of disillusionment. How do you maintain your self-respect without isolating your gifts? Whom can you trust? Where is the love? Should you simply go along to get along? While valid, these questions lead you away from where the focus of your faith formation must lie. For you see, your faith formation has essentially to do with the authority of Jesus Christ, not the fallibility of human beings. Were it not for Jesus, people, especially church folk, would drain us of any capacity to love.

Love Is the Greatest Gift

The ability to remain loving in the face of the seemingly unlovable is one of the most difficult tasks you will ever undertake. Yet the ability to love in spite of is God's greatest commandment to us. Paul's letter to the Corinthian church provides instructions on the true manifestation of love:

What if I could speak
 all languages of humans and of angels?
If I did not love others,
 I would be nothing more
than a noisy gong
 or a clanging cymbal.
What if I could prophesy
and understand all secrets
 and all knowledge?
And what if I had faith
 that moved mountains?
I would be nothing,
 unless I loved others.
What if I gave away all
 that I owned
and let myself
 be burned alive?
I would gain nothing,
 unless I loved others.
Love is kind and patient,
never jealous, boastful,
 proud, or rude.
Love isn't selfish
 or quick tempered.
It doesn't keep a record
 of wrongs that others do.

Love rejoices in the truth,
    but not in evil.
Love is always supportive,
loyal, hopeful,
    and trusting.
Love never fails!

Everyone who prophesies
    will stop,
and unknown languages
will no longer
    be spoken.
All that we know
    will be forgotten.
We don't know everything,
and our prophecies
    are not complete.
But what is perfect
    will someday appear,
and what isn't perfect
    will then disappear.

When we were children,
we thought and reasoned
    as children do.
But when we grew up,
    we quit our childish ways.
Now all we can see of God
is like a cloudy picture
    in a mirror.
Later we will see him
    face to face.
We don't know everything,
    but then we will,
just as God completely
    understands us.

For now there are faith,
*   hope, and love.*
But of these three,
*   the greatest is love.*
(1 Corinthians 13, CEV)

While we are moved by the poetry of Paul's letter, it was not written to touch us aesthetically. Paul's instructions about the true nature of love were written to feuding church folk. The exhortation of 1 Corinthians 13 was intended to show the church at Corinth and show us how far we live from authentic love. Love in Paul's epistle is not the mushy, sugar-coated adrenalin type of love that wears rose-colored glasses; it is real, raw, and unconditional. It awakens supernatural compassion, forgiveness, and flexibility. Examine the attributes of love about which Paul writes: total transparency, complete humility, absolute sacrifice, patience, kindness, endurance, consistency, maturity, harmlessness, vision, grace, forgiveness, and wisdom.

Through the lens of true love, who among us has a life that actively reflects the demands of the text? Yet, Jesus makes this love the standard for righteousness. So you see, it is not just about them—the bubble busters, hypocrites, and deceivers. It is about you. Who are you in the realm of God? What is the quality of your relationship with God? How well do you understand your prophetic purpose? How are you loving?

I remember loving
Loving until my soul was raw
and my mind dissipated.
I remember loving
Loving with such an abandonment of self
that I no longer even had a shadow of my own.
I remember loving
Loving until my dreams were shipwrecked without a sail.
I remember loving
until the torment became my only joy.
Then at long last love
found me, awakened me, healed and restored me.

Love spoke my name,
unleashed my purpose,
gave me the world,
a cross, and
an opal ring.
Love shattered all of my illusions,
mended every broken promise,
and danced me into wonder.
Now I am Love
I am Divine
I am Life.
I am Beauty.

A Time to Heal Our Expectations

We are not expected to minister solely to the lost sheep in the world but also to those who are lost in the flock of God. As you deal with ministering to the lost, whether in or out of the church, allow the Word of God to keep your heart from cynicism and your thoughts free of all bitterness. In time, you will realize that not all church folk are hypocrites or lazy or lack a moral compass. You must pray for those that are to return to God. Beyond that, you are responsible only for engaging in a spiritual practice that will grow and mature your faith.

Because your expectations of church folk have become jaded, your enthusiasm has been squelched. Therefore, I offer you a spiritual discipline designed to heal your expectations. A wounded heart can no longer experience beauty. I want you to write your way into wellness through the discipline of spiritual journaling. Unlike a diary, which captures feelings, a journal spiritually requires you to be guided by Christ consciousness. As you write, you will develop a command of Scripture and a strong prayer life. And I believe that your joy will once again be full. And your heart will once again be ablaze with songs of beauty. Journal as though you have nothing to lose and everything to gain. Journal like a woman inebriated with love; like an ocean in a hurricane; like a mystery before dawn; like a baby entering the birth canal.

*"No, the word is very near to you; it is in your mouth
and in your heart for you to observe."
(Deuteronomy 30:14, NRSV)*

Ground Rules for Spiritual Journaling

You may have kept a journal before. However, because spiritual journaling requires a different mindset, let me suggest that you look at the process anew. First, spiritual journaling is not a literary exercise; it is an exercise in praying, in communion with God, the results of which are written. Therefore, do not concern yourself with grammar, punctuation, spelling, or the number of pages you write. The quality of your journaling is determined solely by the power of your engagement with the Holy Spirit. When you go to the page, do not bring an agenda or have an ulterior motive. Listen without encumbrance. Listening is the better part of your assignment.

Those of us who engage in spiritual journaling do not perceive ourselves as writers but as prayer warriors who are willing to risk everything for God's favor. Therefore, the journaling process contains a balance between reflection, meditation, and writing. The following components will render your prayer journaling more and more effective as you are consistent in your practice. Make sure you are free to dedicate at least twenty minutes of quiet time before you begin the process.

Invoke the presence of God. In the name of Jesus, invite the Holy Ghost to be with you, to guide and counsel you and fill you with the fullness of God.

Listen to God. Use images of Calvary to quiet your mind. Let godly stillness overtake your body and emotions.

Write. As the flow of light begins, write what is given to you just as it comes. No need to edit or spiritualize.

Closure. End with the Lord's Prayer. This will preserve your heart from error and give you clarity for living.

Do not be surprised. The glory of this experience will overflow into your marriage. Your tone, temperament, attitude, and, most of all, your worship will enter a new dimension. Consistent practice of one or more of the spiritual disciplines will stretch you. You will begin to hunger deeply for the things of God.

As you journal, you will not only see God but also will begin to glimpse your inner self. You will be able to discern when a shift occurs in your soul. You will reach a point when who you are is no longer who you were! You will begin to live your life to the glory of God.

O God, my heart is fixed; I will sing and give praise, even with my glory. (Psalm 108:1, KJV)

Prayer journaling is a powerful experience, one beloved of the mystic and the novice. Respect the process. Your pen may recall for you portions of Scripture, sermons, or songs. She may lead you to closed doors or open windows, to solve mysteries or create a conundrum. Whatever it may be, respect the process.

As you journal, you will not only see God but also begin to glimpse your inner self. You will be able to discern when a shift occurs in your soul. Again, you will reach a point when who you are is no longer who you were!

O God, my heart is fixed; I will sing and give praise, even with my glory. (Psalm 108:1, KJV)

Your pen may capture both prophetic and apocalyptic visions. The following provides additional recommendations for making the most of journaling.

The Prophetic Pen

"Write down what you have seen."
(Revelation 1:19, NLT)

The prophetic pen writes revelations and messages received from the Holy Spirit. Therefore, as you write, do not censor or attempt to interpret the message that comes to you. Rather, simply serve as a scribe. Record thoughts, images, words, names, revelations, and Scriptures. Whatever comes, write it down!

Let the name of Jesus be the thread that holds all things together as you open yourself to receive his presence. Invoking the name of

Jesus can shatter all darkness, and the Light of revelation will shine in you and can radically change your presence on the earth. Be mindful that a still pen is not necessarily an indication of the silence of God. Remain present in the Presence. Light often comes even as a quiet knowing. In time, you may become aware of themes emerging as you journal. Do not speak too quickly or openly about what you receive. You may begin to know the voice of God in a different way. Allow prayer to lead, and your pen will follow.

The Apocalyptic Pen

"tongues of mortals and of angels. . . ."
(1 Corinthians 13:1, NRSV)

The apocalyptic pen records visions and signs received from the supernatural realm. The Holy Spirit not only speaks in word, in languages known and unknown to the disciple, but also in sound, images, symbols, and supernatural visions. These also must be recorded. Very often we must use anthropomorphic references to write about things that have no earthly likeness. Ezekiel saw and wrote of dry bones in a valley. Such things are too great for human wit and wisdom to understand without the power of God. What you see in prayer does not have to make sense! There are many signs of God's realm that may remain beyond our understanding.

Praying in the Spirit brings clarity and centeredness to our lives, thus freeing us of all pretensions and healing our vulnerabilities. Envisioning the things of God can evoke fresh nuances in our faith formation, causing us to move into another realm of living, speaking, and understanding. For those mature in this spiritual discipline, the evidence of this movement is neither boisterous nor showy, but rather, profoundly humbling.

Discernment

For now we see through a glass, darkly.
(1 Corinthians 13:12, KJV)

In the fullness of God's time, God makes known to us the will and purposes of the kingdom. The way we must go, with whom we shall journey, and that which we must speak—all these become clearer to us. Note that not all the dimensions of your prophetic purpose will be known to you. God is always doing a work in us, always confronting us with a greater light than we now possess.

Because we lack complete understanding, we must pray at all times to be led by the Spirit of the Lord. "Those who are spiritual discern all things, and they are themselves subject to no one else's scrutiny . . . [because] we have the mind of Christ" (1 Corinthians 2:15-16, NRSV).

Our task is to depend upon the Word of God to discern the "thoughts and intentions of the heart" (Hebrews 4:12, NRSV). As you develop the spiritual discipline of journaling, it is essential that you regularly read and meditate upon the Scriptures, especially the Wisdom literature of Psalms and Proverbs. Wisdom will help to keep you grounded so that the enemy remains under your feet!

Journaling and Incarnation

I put away childish things. (1 Corinthians 13:11, KJV)

By godly submission and faithfulness we are empowered to write ourselves whole. As a word revealed to us is manifested in us, we, too, become the living Word. We take our focus off people and give God our full attention. Like the prophets before us, we are not exempt from humiliation, attack, emotional exhaustion, or frustration. Yet the Word demands unconditional fidelity. The Word that once brooded within you leaps off the pages into your soul psyche, detaching you from every other consideration, preference, and issue. The Word in you has become the Light surrounding you.

For once you were darkness, but now in the Lord you are light. Live as children of light. (Ephesians 5:8, NRSV)

The Glorious Expectation

When that which is perfect is come. . . .
(1 Corinthians 13:10, KJV)

We die to write away our embarrassments, shortcomings, indiscretions, fears, loneliness, and misjudgments. We die to write ourselves happy. Like Moses, we want to see God's face. But when that which is perfect has come, all lesser expectations of promotion, prosperity, and gifts crumble. The writer is divinely connected with both the unseen and the tangible. When the pen is laid to rest, the evidence must show undeniably that you have been with God! We understand, in this instance, that to write is to pray because we know that our God is Word indeed. God is the living, incarnate, and eternal Word. And so, we write to spend time with God. We are servant writers, scribes of resurrection immersed in the articulation of the mystery.

Discouragement has the power to cripple the growth of the soul. Take courage again from the knowledge that you are loved, that the sun will rise, that music is eternal, that you are indeed God's woman.

Take courage again from your awareness of the presence of the Lord, the truth of the holy sacraments, the living Word, the beauty of holiness, and the rest that the sabbath brings.

Take courage again from your prophetic pen, your pen of consolation, your apocalyptic pen, your pen of healing, your pen of glorious expectation.

And so, dear Zion, the perfection that you seek will not be found in yourself or others. The perfection you seek is that Word that was in the beginning, is now, and ever shall be! You may pardon with your pen those who have disappointed you, including yourself. Allow the omniscient, omnipresent, omnipotent Word to invade your thinking and feeling and believing. Holiness will surely shine within your soul. Beauty and favor will lie at your feet because you have given yourself to love. The Word cannot die. The living Word is the answer to every question, the solution to every conflict, the very root of prophetic purpose.

Love never fails. (1 Corinthians 13:8, NKJV)

LETTER 5

Ophir
Ambition

"Instead, whoever wants to become great among you must be
your servant, and whoever wants to be first must be your slave—
just as the Son of Man did not come to be served, but to serve."
(Matthew 20:26-28, NIV)

Dear Ophir,

Your husband did not enter the ministry to get rich but to enrich
the lives of others. While God desires you to prosper as you minister, your sole desire should be to lead souls to Christ and meet the
needs of people. What is your understanding of the gospel? You
seem to have fallen victim to the seduction of prosperity thinking.

The fact that your husband obtained a seminary education does
not guarantee him a six-figure income, an annual cruise, or a full-
time housekeeper. His pursuit of education indicates that he is
committed to ministry and desires to give God the very best. In
addition to being well-educated, your husband is compassionate,
generous, hardworking, and highly regarded among his peers.
More than that, he is totally devoted to you.

Despite all of his virtues, you have assigned yourself the task of
comparing him with others, downplaying his progress, and cam-
paigning to elevate him and yourself. Please know that a marriage
wherein the wife consistently communicates to her husband that
he is weak, inadequate, unsuccessful, and lagging behind cannot

last long. It is time you discovered what is missing within you that you would put your marriage under such pressure.

Authentic covenant clergy marriage is lived according to God's time, principles, and purpose. Much is required, and much is given. The key is to discover those things that are of kingdom value and how God is calling you to live out God's will for your marriage. Work with what you have been given. Leave the results to God. The worst thing you can do is covet someone else's results while rejecting your spouse's gifts and the authentic gift God has given you.

The gifts he gave were that some would be apostles, some prophets, some evangelists, some pastors and teachers, to equip the saints for the work of ministry, for building up the body of Christ. (Ephesians 4:11-12, NRSV)

The Lord has given us these gifts. It is God who has chosen the vessel. The recipient of the gifts is required to act faithfully and with integrity. Your husband demonstrates both in his ministry. The only thing that prevents him from enjoying his ministry is your selfish ambition, which suggests to him that his best just isn't good enough!

Right now you are living in the wilderness. More than that, the wilderness lives within you. But the good news is that God's voice can be heard even in the wilderness. There is only one way through and out of the wilderness: you must examine yourself.

As crazy as this may sound, I do believe that you really do love the man! But you must love him! "*Ecco homo,*" as the Scripture says, "Behold the man." See him! See his soul, his vision, his longing. Love him. Not a fantasized version of him. Don't wrap him in a Benny Hinn, Billy Graham, fluorescent light cloak and expect him to shine. Behold Christ in him and *rejoice*!

Your spiritual formation has been thwarted by the seductive power of that which is external and material. For you, Sunday mornings have been reduced to a grand entrance and a dramatic departure. Because you have a higher calling, you must take the time to learn the voice and authentic ways of God. Get in touch with your own spirituality. Your own prophetic purpose. Your own gifting. I recommend, therefore, the spiritual discipline of examen.

The Spiritual Discipline of Examen

"You will know the truth, and the truth will make you free." (John 8:32, NRSV)

As disciples of Jesus Christ, we owe it to God and to ourselves to look into our souls with the light of God's Word. It is possible to love God and be erroneous in our witness. Even though you have received eternal life, you continue to perpetrate confusion. Examen is a spiritual discipline that directs its practitioner to reflect on his or her life. It requires its practitioner to become aware of motivations and unhealthy ways of interacting. Once examined, the practitioner can create a new future. You are strong. You are bold. You have what it takes to make this vision quest come alive.

"Open their eyes so they may turn from darkness to light, and from the power of Satan to God. Then they will receive forgiveness for their sins and be given a place among God's people, who are set apart by faith in me." (Acts 26:18, NLT)

Start the practice of examen by asking yourself how you have been living the past few years. It is time you stopped, looked at your life, and discerned your motives. We are all broken vessels, but we can be put back together again. Trust that God's love is available to you right now just as you are. As you practice examen, do not consider yourself a defendant in a court case; rather, see yourself as a soul on a quest for godliness. View yourself as an empty vessel who desires the fullness of divine communion.

As you engage in examen, hold a mirror to your life. Pray to see the woman God sees as you look through the lens of Scripture. Ask yourself the following questions: What is the true source of my motivation? What do I really value in life? What energy do I release in the universe? What is my life purpose? Who have I harmed in word or deed? God may place other questions on your heart. Neither your questions nor your answers need to be precise. Pray to dislodge any emotional, spiritual, or personality road blocks to wholeness. Trust the Holy Spirit to keep your heart as you embrace this very sensitive process. Do not push yourself beyond what you can bear in any one setting. Stop to give yourself some healing space before re-entering the process. Know that examen must be an open, ongoing spiritual discipline. Therefore, do not attempt to superimpose artificial deadlines on your progress. From now on, you have the power to initiate restoration by the daily decisions you make.

Psalm 26:2 (NIV) offers you a wonderful morning prayer:

Test me, O LORD, and try me,
  examine my heart and my mind.

Keep this supplication before you as you go throughout the day.
I believe that it will create a shift in your temperament and attitude.

Once you have entered the process and are familiar with the rhythm of examen, I recommend that you set aside a day for a personal at-home retreat, an eight-hour day of complete solitude and prayer. Below are my suggestions for planning and implementing a one-day retreat.

Let us examine our ways and test them,
  and let us return to the LORD.
  (Lamentations 3:40, NIV)

For an eight-hour period, you will spend time alone communicating only with God. During this day, you will confront and purge the wilderness within you. Anticipate new freedom, new joy, new peace, new hope, fresh enthusiasm.

Preparation

Freedom from distraction will assure you of optimum results. Do not sabotage yourself. You know what you have to do. Look upon this day as an adventure with God. It is not a day of punishment. Be open to the process. In preparation for your day of retreat, do the following the day before:

- Have on hand soup, garden salad, fruit, yogurt, herbal tea, and mineral water to carry you through the day.
- Meditate on Matthew 4:1-11 the night before, as your day's process will center on this text.
- Refrain from watching television.
- Gather the following items: a Bible, a journal, and a prayer cushion or rug.
- Jot down questions you want to ask yourself or to which you want answers.

Retreat Process

Each segment of the day is broken into two-hour slots and has a specific prayer and scriptural focus. Yet, infuse the day with your own creativity. Make it as luxurious or as austere as suits your case.

Segment 1: Prayer focus on submission

> Then Jesus was led up by the Spirit. (Matthew 4:1, NKJV)

The first portion of your day should be spent in a posture of submission. Pray the Holy Spirit to guide your thoughts. If you begin to experience "self" consciousness, resistance, anger, or any other distraction, renounce them in the name of Jesus. Ponder what it is you have submitted to in your life. Is it wealth? Fame? Superiority? Whatever it is, ask the Holy Spirit to remove it from the altar of your heart. As you submit, talk to God with your pen, in song, in tears, or in silence. Meditate on Psalms 29, 42, and 131 during this period. Embrace the lyrics of this hymn by Judson W. Van DeVenter (1896):

All to Jesus I surrender;
All to Him I freely give;
I will ever love and trust Him,
In His presence daily live.
 I surrender all,
 I surrender all.
 All to Thee, my blessed Savior,
 I surrender all.

Segment 2: Prayer focus on reflection

"It is written." (Matthew 4:4, 7, 10, NKJV)

The wilderness is a place of uncertainty, vulnerability, and self-doubt. It is nowhere to build a marriage. You have tainted your marriage with a host of questions regarding your husband's ministry. You have questioned his calling, his anointing, even his love for you, just because he does not share your desire for great material prosperity.

Therefore, you should spend the second portion of your retreat in deep reflection. Use this time to reflect on whether those thoughts originate in your heart or some other place. Reflect on what would happen if you allowed yourself to be happy with the life you now live. What impact would it have on you, your husband, and the ministry? During this segment, meditate on Psalms 39, 40, and 41. Allow each word to enter your heart. You may also choose to walk or practice tai chi or yoga as you reflect, allowing your body to release tension.

Segment 3: Prayer focus on repentance and release

During this next two hours, you should engage in repentance and release. The following steps will help lead to repentance and release:

- Pray the Holy Spirit to remind you of recent occasions, conversations, and behaviors in which you engaged that were unworthy of a child of God. Ask the Holy Spirit to teach you words and actions that will bring reconciliation.
- Pray the Lord God to minister restoration to your marriage and impart a sense of grace and humility in your communication with your husband.

- Ask God to forgive your sins. Vow to ask forgiveness of those you have injured. Weep for the sins you have committed against your marriage. Vow never to forsake the Word of God in your heart, soul, and mind.
- Conclude with a season of silence, letting this psalm resonate in your spirit:

Then I realized how bitter I had become,
   how pained I had been by all I had seen.
I was so foolish and ignorant—
   I must have seemed like a senseless animal to you. . . .
Whom have I in heaven but you?
   I desire you more than anything on earth.
   —Psalm 73:21-22, 25 (NLT)

Segment 4: Prayer focus on consecration

"Worship the Lord your God, and serve him only."
(Matthew 4:10, NIV)

Consecration is what distinguishes authentic discipleship from church membership. It is the decision made in faith to live wholly for God. The cult of prosperity is silent on this matter. Too often those who promote the social gospel get lost in their issues. Pew guardians have only personal power in mind. Yet, looming in our midst is the cross of Calvary demanding a response. Consecration asks the question, "Are you willing to let it *all* go for the sake of the redeeming love of Jesus Christ?" The hesitation, the silence, the compromise resound through our witness and ministry.

To live a life of consecration
I renounce and release:
Rage, in the name of Jesus
Pride, in the name of Jesus
Materialism, in the name of Jesus
Jealousy, in the name of Jesus
Self-indulgence, in the name of Jesus
Fear, in the name of Jesus
   In the name of Jesus

In the name of Jesus
In the name of Jesus
"Let us approach with a true heart
in full assurance of faith,
with our hearts sprinkled clean
from an evil conscience . . ." (Hebrews 10:22, NRSV)

Now that you have released the negative forces from your life, you are ready to chart a new direction. Use the following as your guide:

- Begin a life of daily prayer.
- Commit to attend Bible study.
- Become a consistent tither.
- Develop relationships with happy clergy spouses.
- Initiate a ministry in your church or community that meets the needs of people.
- Encourage spouses serving at churches smaller than yours.
- Speak blessings into your husband's life, health, and ministry, and seek effective ways to serve with him.

While a personality over forty years in the making will not be transformed in a day, it can be refocused. Nor can a marital pattern of relationship that is the product of nearly fifteen years be erased in eight hours. Nevertheless, God promises to perfect that which concerns us. We have only to begin.

It is not often that we have the opportunity to begin again. Once you have become fully engaged in the practice of examen, schedule an intimate evening with your husband to renew your vows to each other. Covenant clergy marriage is God's opportunity to renew the earth and to establish the kingdom of heaven. A marriage lived for God will receive the treasure of the kingdom. There will be days less glorious than your wedding day. But you will discover that God gives grace even for ordinary days. Seize this opportunity to refocus your light, and you will become a blessed blessing.

LETTER 6

Lappidoth

Husband as Pastor's Spouse

Deborah, a prophetess, the wife of Lappidoth,
was leading Israel at that time.
(Judges 4:4, NIV)

Dear Lappidoth,

Despite pivotal strides in gender equality, we still live in a man's world. Vestiges of this disturbing antiquity remain in the African American church in ways that are unhealthy to say the least! A pastor's spouse is presumed to be a woman, and in most instances still is. However, you are among a growing number of men whose wives are pastors. Because few men have journeyed along this path, you are bound to face this role with a level of discomfort and ambivalence.

Sunday after Sunday, you watch as your wife stands behind the holy desk representing an all-powerful God through the power of the Holy Spirit. You are a member of the congregation that is under her authority. You cannot help but perceive your wife as powerful. But then you go home with her where tradition says you are in charge. Power struggles abound in all marriages with respect to decision making, finances, sex, or authority. However, the power issues in your marriage may be exacerbated by your wife's position. It is vitally important, therefore, that you create a decision-making process that affirms both of you and your marriage. The God of reconciliation and compassion must be your

eternal source of humility and balance. You can lay claim to all of
the biblical promises of grace and empowerment.

Remember, you are among an elect circle of men who experience firsthand the passion and divinity of the bed and board of
God's prophet. You spend your life with a woman whose very
nature defies conventional marriage. Yet in true covenant clergy
marriage, where God is in charge, she comes alive.

You are honored. And both of you remain whole. Somehow,
our wedding vows never quite capture the real dynamic of human
vulnerabilities. We float down the aisle oblivious to the emotional
land mines, past traumas, and unplanned frustrations that await
us. Today you are God's. You are man. You are chosen. Embrace
it, and see what delight the kingdom takes in your faithfulness.

But for you who revere my name the sun of
righteousness shall rise, with healing in its wings.
(Malachi 4:2, NRSV)

The Glory of Covenant Clergy Marriage

Place me like a seal over your heart,
    like a seal on your arm;
for love is as strong as death,
    its jealousy unyielding as the grave.
It burns like blazing fire,
    like a mighty flame.
Many waters cannot quench love;
    rivers cannot wash it away.
If one were to give
    all the wealth of his house for love,
    it would be utterly scorned.
    —Song of Solomon 8:6-7 (NIV)

Covenant clergy marriage is God's vision for our life together in the
presence of the Lord. Our maleness and femaleness are sacred con-
texts that enunciate the mystery, magic, and music of our union.
Our souls are adrift until we discover the light in one another.
When God reigns in the relationship between husband and wife,

the mystical and the mundane begin to exude a special quality that is difficult to articulate or define. Yet, it is too real to be denied.

Let me say on your wife's behalf, "You are the man!" Embrace it! Let the reality of it speak to you in all of your vulnerable places. Because God has established it, you don't have to prove it! Let your husbanding be manifested in your intercession, encouragement, and the ways in which you make love to her. Know that God has not betrayed you by creating you male and calling your wife to preach the gospel any more than the favor of Mary was the attempt of a capricious deity to humiliate Joseph!

This is purely a spiritual matter. I know it may not seem so when the members of the church volunteer you to be janitor and van driver and to work with the boys. The less glorious tasks of the kingdom are so often unkindly and unfairly imposed upon all clergy spouses. The privacy that is so precious to you has become nonexistent. Strangers who take the liberty to get in your business are disconcerting. Yet, in every experience, life is teaching us something about God, ourselves, and love. To be a disciple is to be one who is taught. Our most powerful life lessons are those that stretch our imaginations and enhance our personalities. Surely, a congregation is an academy in crisis management.

Despite the many challenges and inconveniences, there is a way to maintain your testimony as a disciple of Jesus Christ that frees you of the manipulation and insensitivity of mortal pride. Following the way will prevent resentment and bitterness from seeping into your marriage. It is within this mystery that your husbanding becomes holy, irresistible, and perfect. The Scriptures say we are not our own (see 1 Corinthians 6:19). Husbanding plumbs the depths of this revelation. With God and the woman, you co-create, co-labor, and bring light to the world.

As you engage the role of the clergy spouse, I encourage you to walk a pathway to the heart of God that has the power to dismantle insecurity, pride, unforgiveness, and all else that is at war with covenant clergy marriage. This spiritual discipline is known as centering prayer. Centering prayer allows you to pursue the Spirit of the Lord without the sensation of falling off a cliff. You may be overwhelmed, your body exhausted, your emotions drained. Yet, you are about to enter a path of restoration, one in which you will receive clarity and fresh enthusiasm. But to sustain your inner peace as a clergy spouse, your heart must be centered in prayer.

If it is not possible for you to slow down, you must stop and recenter. When you stop, when you let go, you acknowledge that God is in control, so you don't have to be. God is sovereign; you will never be. Shatter the myth of the culture that drives you to prove your manhood. Accept the freedom that comes with knowing that it is God who justifies. This freedom translates into a prayer life without regulations or formulas. One that is not trapped by dogma or tradition. A prayer life in which you can go to God without baggage. Centering prayer precipitates a change in your very being. You must become open, susceptible, and yielded to a new move of God, a fresh wind from the throne room. Communion with God is a sacred privilege offered to every Christian. It is not reserved for those who are ordained. Be courageous, and consent to a journey that will heal the quality of your life.

Unleashing the Power of Centering Prayer

Centering prayer will return your soul to love, awaken your divine consciousness, and illumine you with the radiance of God. You will live within the holiness of God's realm. It is only through holiness that God can protect a marriage from debilitating pride, syncretism, materialistic idolatry, and parasitic boredom. The marital relationship must not be reduced to that of colleagues, housemates, or simply companions. Indeed, so sacred is marriage that it is a parable for the kingdom of God. By unleashing the power of centering prayer, by coming into the presence of the Lord, your healing is assured, and your marriage will reign in sacred passion. You see, prayer is not passive. We prevail in prayer as we allow our consciousness of God to become unboundaried, when we free ourselves of ritual, vocabulary, and posture.

"When you are praying, do not heap up empty phrases."
(Matthew 6:7, NRSV)

There are times when our most effectual praying is wordless. Yet, the outpouring of our souls speaks volumes to the heart of God. Simply yield to the love of the divine presence.

The Practice of Centering Prayer

The African American prayer culture tends to be passionate and lyrical and engages others while seeking the Lord. Centering prayer requires an inward shift that is a departure from that tradition. It invites us to be separated, physically where possible, and to be engaged only by God. To practice centering prayer, you must withdraw the power of your thoughts and imagination from everything except the knowledge that God loves you! Let God's love rest upon your heart and quiet all anxieties. When fully embraced, the reality of God's love descends to the very center of your soul.

The following experience will provide a glimpse into centering prayer—

> While kneeling before a statue of the crucified Jesus,
>   my soul became wrapped in the silence of God.
> I was led by the Holy Spirit to prostrate myself.
> And, as I lay there, my heart ablaze with the love of God,
> I experienced myself as pure Spirit.
> Neither time, or place, or the contours of my own body
>   possessed any reality for me.
> I was no longer the woman who had entered the cathedral.
>   I had become a cathedral.
> Hallelujah!

Instructions for the Practice of Centering Prayer

As preparation, allow yourself thirty minutes of uninterrupted time. Separate yourself physically and emotionally from others.

Sit in a comfortable posture. Take the time to breathe your body into relaxation. Acknowledge Emmanuel, God who is with us. You will know that you are safe. Quietly take in your surroundings.

Step 1: Close your eyes and whisper the Lord's Prayer to the rhythm of your breath. Repeat as necessary to attain inner stillness.

Step 2: Inhale deeply. As you exhale, "God loves me!" Pray this continuously as the Spirit of the Lord directs.

Step 3: As the Holy Spirit leads you, begin to honor the attributes of God until prayer becomes your breathing.

Step 4: Listen to the heart of God.

As the Spirit leads you to closure, whisper or sing the doxology. Slowly open your eyes and wait until you are ready to stand.

Let my prayer be counted as incense before you. (Psalm 141:2, NRSV)

As you are mastered by centering prayer, your body will release the tension caused by a life that is off-center. Your heart will unlock, your shoulders will relax, your stomach will quiet, and your breathing will become more fluid. You will be overtaken by the amazing peace of God. Your reality has not changed, but you have. You are still a man married to a powerful woman of God. Circumstances are no different. You still may be called to coach the church softball team on top of everything else! But, you are different.

I will give you the treasures of darkness
and riches hidden in secret places,
so that you may know that it is I, the Lord,
the God of Israel, who calls you by your name.
—Isaiah 45:3 (NRSV)

Once we disengage the notion of intimacy from the erotic connotations that the culture attaches to it, what remains is a phenomena that is glorious in spiritual impact. To be the beloved is a gender-free confession. It is to resonate, inwardly, with the highest degree of spiritual passion. It is a grounding transcendence, an epiphany of grace. It is to know Love.

With this awareness, from deep within, begin to extol and adore the character of God. You will experience God as **holy, com-**

passionate, mysterious, just, merciful, righteous, the light, the truth, love, even life itself. Allow your soul to abide in each of these attributes of God. As a son of God, each of these ten attributes must be manifested in you and in your marriage. If areas of your life are in conflict with these divine attributes, seek through prayer to bring them into submission. Maintain your center. Your interior sanctuary demands humility and reverence. Although these qualities may be countercultural with regard to manliness, they develop strength and integrity of character. You will begin to manifest your manhood in supernatural ways; as a husband, you will be a source of healing and joy.

> *This is the message we have heard from him and declare to you: God is light; in him there is no darkness at all. (1 John 1:5, NIV)*

Covenant marriage comes with a unique biblical freedom clause: "Be subject to one another out of reverence for Christ" (Ephesians 5:21, NIV), which effectively dismantles the system of hierarchy in the marital relationship. In Christ we are liberated to one another. For the conclusion of the matter is this: "we are members of his body" (Ephesians 5:30, NIV).

As we discover the authentic Christ meaning in marriage, we become a rhapsody of grace. For there is no more beautiful light than the light of the countenance of one who has been resurrected by Love. It's a life worth praying for. It is a life with eternity poured into it.

> *He was a devout man who feared God with all his household; he gave alms generously to the people and prayed constantly to God. (Acts 10:2, NRSV)*

As you pursue a life of centering prayer, know that you will experience a healing of your perspective, your vulnerabilities, and your spiritual reluctance. Other men will be magnetized by your faith, and your spiritual gifting will flourish.

Let your marriage be shaped by this sacred unfolding. All power belongs to God. As God imparts to us wisdom and anointing, we are free to develop a system of collaboration and mutuality befitting children of God. Our finances, parenting, time, priorities, and leisure are a reflection of the concerns of both husband and wife. Having said this, when it comes to the ministry, each of us must live out our faith in ways that glorify God.

When you engage in centering prayer, you are also engaged by it. Centering prayer takes effort. Though you are required to be still, you must also be completely engaged within! A life of doing has sent so many of us away from ourselves without understanding who we are, whose we are, or our prophetic purpose. As disciples, lay and clergy, God calls each of us to communion and rest. You are uniquely positioned by God for great kingdom impact. The thought of being a role model or leader may be more than you bargained for.

"Do not be afraid or discouraged. For the LORD your God is with you wherever you go." (Joshua 1:9, NLT).

Remember Barak, Joseph, and the husbands of Rosa Parks, C. Delores Tucker, Bishop Vashti McKenzie, Bishop Sarah Francis Davis, and Maxine Waters. Remember and be refreshed.

Praying does not allow us to escape life's challenges but rather to delve into them in the power of the Holy Spirit. The greater part of centering prayer is to experience the freedom of release. Release from all negativity as we await the revelation of God. We wait knowing that love waits with us. You can wait with God only if you trust God's compassion and mercy. That same divine compassion and mercy are essential for healthy covenant clergy marriage. This is not to gloss over the natural concerns, challenges, joys, or frustrations. But in covenant clergy marriage, God is the third party to the contract. Therefore, neither husband nor wife can give place to darkness. Instead, each agrees that the eternal light of the kingdom will shine in them for better or worse, in sickness and health until parted by death.

The light of God shapes the path we must journey. It is not the terrain that makes the marriage but the covenant that masters the terrain. Do not permit yourself to wander away from the light by your thoughts, attitude, or behavior.

Centering prayer invokes a climate of grace capable of diffusing tension and frustration.

Centering prayer is conducive to any situation.

Centering prayer empowers one to disengage from conflict.

Centering prayer opens the way to fresh insight.

Centering prayer promotes health.

Centering prayer brings refreshing.

Centering prayer maintains your awareness of the presence of the Lord.

One of the benefits of communicating with God is that our communication with others is transformed. Not only our words but our thoughts are healed by the Light.

A heart centered in prayer not only listens but also receives new ways of hearing. Therefore, hear the heart of your wife without defense, and share your heart with her without condemnation. Soon it will no longer be a matter of being right or in control. Your concern will be that you are facing the future together with God. That your marriage is not oppressed by insecurity or rivalry.

Show kindness in your husbanding. Husbanding is the covering of the Lord over your household. To husband is to be the ark of safety—psychological, physical, spiritual, and artistic. Every marriage has need of such. To husband is to inspire, to affirm, to imagine, to heal, and to seek eternity together with the spouse of your covenant. When suffering comes—and it will—your marriage will endure. By the power of the Holy Spirit, you and your consecrated wife become a force for the kingdom of God, an unstoppable, tangible expression of love that has no end.

> *Then our mouth was filled with laughter,*
> *and our tongue with shouts of joy.*
> —*Psalm 126:2 (NRSV)*

LETTER 7

Mahalath

Stress

You, LORD, give true peace.
>   You give peace to those who depend on you.
>   You give peace to those who trust you.
So, trust the LORD always.
>   Trust the LORD because he is our Rock forever.
—Isaiah 26:3-4 (NCV)

Akwaba Mahalath (Welcome, Gracious One)!

Come back to yourself! No one can maintain the dizzying pace that has become the norm for you without falling completely out of balance. You are brilliant, compassionate, discerning, effective, and creative. Yet your countenance reads, "Do not approach me; I am preoccupied." That's because the only opportunity you have to sit down is at church on Sunday morning. By that time, you have nothing left to give of yourself, not a smile, a warm hand-shake, a gesture of awareness, or a word of encouragement. Your role of first lady is completely devoid of your personhood. But this is only a symptom of a larger problem: unabated stress.

As a wife, mother, executive, and cultural icon, you have worked hard to achieve the current level of stress in your life. Unfortunately, stress has the power to corrupt personality, dimin-ish character, create disease, and alter discernment. Stress has trou-bled your appetite and digestive system, marred your beautiful complexion, and silenced your libido. You are well aware of this. Yet, you haven't been able to stop yourself.

The journey that has led to the level of stress in your life has been both productive and alienating. Being among the who's who has cost you your well-being and spiritual focus. The beauty of covenant clergy marriage is that it provides endless opportunities to be at the center of a move of God on behalf of God's people. We are able to see and foresee the transforming power of the gospel. We ride the vision from conception through turmoil to manifestation. And, if we are intentional, we will have the grace and the desire to counsel, cheer, challenge, and cuddle one another along the way. But as we give our all for the cause of Christ, we can stress ourselves out. Regrettably, you have silenced the voice of the Spirit while paying homage to the voices crying "success," "wealth," "fame." You are rapidly losing touch with your marriage and vocation, even as you soar in splendid, albeit stressful, isolation.

Wisdom teaches us to create space for love, to prevent busyness from suffocating our mystical union so that we will know when it's time to rest. But at times we fail to heed wisdom. When you think it over, how much of your psychological and creative energy has been devoted to your marriage? How often are you in intercession for your spouse? How much time do you devote to self-care? Please do not allow this inquiry to become another source of stress! Rather, let it serve to challenge you to re-create your world in the images of peace, tranquility, contentment, and passion. Life can be beautiful, exhilarating, and fun. We have the power to decide daily the measure and the quality of our lives.

◆

He has made everything beautiful in its time. He has also set eternity in the hearts of men; yet they cannot fathom what God has done from beginning to end. (Ecclesiastes 3:11, NIV)

I know of your deep love for our Lord and your desire that the church manifest God's favor. Yet, consumed by stress and the need to be perfect, you have lost sight of what is really important. I encourage you to reclaim yourself for the Lord. I invite you to advance your spiritual formation by offering your life as an oblation, a gift for God. Allow everything in your life to be shaped by the reality that you are God's gift. There are so many ways that you can effortlessly bless the people of God by pouring your gifts into the lives of others. But you must first restore your strength, reignite your fire, and heal your own wounds. Give God your emptiness, and allow the light of God's grace to lead you to healing waters.

> "The LORD bless you
>   and keep you;
> the LORD make his face shine upon you
>   and be gracious to you;
> the LORD turn his face toward you
>   and give you peace."
> —Numbers 6:24-26 (NIV)

The Path of the Oblate

"But I am sending you to say to them, 'This is what the Sovereign LORD says!' And whether they listen or not—for remember, they are rebels—at least they will know they have had a prophet among them." (Ezekiel 2:4-5, NLT)

The oblate person does not fear or seek anonymity; she knows her own name. Nor does she have a need to call attention to herself. The light of Jesus Christ shines in her life, and she is both transparent and translucent. For her, Christ is all. To become an oblate, she must travel the path of humility. This path requires letting go of the obsession with control and perfection, the fear of failure and vulnerability; letting go of the mistrust of others and shadows of the past; letting go of resistance to the unknown. The call of the oblate is one without ambiguity. It is definite, prevailing, and soul engaging. It hears God's voice in every inflection, nuance, and whisper. With the clarity of thunder, the consolation of warm milk, and the beauty of a garden in summer, even the chastisement of the Lord tastes of honey. The call of God brings intention and freedom, purpose and balance, rest and energy to a soul preoccupied and overwrought.

The Act of Prostration

O come, let us worship and bow down.
(Psalm 95:6, KJV)

In searching the Scriptures, you will discover that both mortals and angels bow down when they are in the presence of the most high God. Prostration is a sign of submission, reverence, and worship that takes you out of yourself—your priorities, position, and control. When you prostrate yourself, you engage your soul life at the deepest level. You shift your vision from earth to glory. You penetrate authentic reality.

Prostration is a powerful act of oblation. It is the place where the soul is emptied and can be filled. In this place you allow yourself to experience the end of all things and you are simply breath and light. You are free to think only of paradise, glory, and heaven.

To give yourself back to God, lie before your altar with your forehead touching the floor. Extend your arms as though in crucifixion and begin to pray in the power of the Holy Spirit the pilgrim's prayer:

Lord Jesus Christ,
Son of the living God,
have mercy upon me.

Pray until your only thought or desire is to remain in the presence of the Light until no other words except spontaneous adoration enter your thoughts or pass through your lips. Begin to experience all anxiety passing away as the peace of God settles upon you. Make your prostration daily as often as the spirit leads you. You will know when God is speaking to you. You will be taught how to prioritize your time and relationships. You will begin to trace the movement of divine love in your personality.

As you engage in prostration, make the following affirmations:

When I lay prostrate, I am symbolically emptying myself
of all darkness, and I say:

Jesus is the Light of the world.
Jesus is the Light of my life.
Jesus is the Light.
When I lay prostrate, the light in me is surrendering
    to the greater Light, Jesus Christ, Son of God.
When I lay prostrate, I transition from a self-centered
    to a Christ-centered consciousness.
When I lay prostrate, I create an interior chapel of prayer.
When I lay prostrate, a shroud of silence covers me.
When I lay prostrate, I enter the freedom of God.

Sanctification is the path of the oblate. Sanctification is never instantaneous; it is a process. We who have issues such as resistance, perfectionism, and impatience will experience acute frustration. We may have to measure our time in three-hour segments rather than twenty-four hours. So be it. Love is the destination, the path, and the power. Each prostration must answer the call to love. Know that the time for prostration has come when your thoughts are dominated by negative energy. The time has come when there is tension or resentment erupting in your marriage. There is a cure for what ails you—be the love.

Prostration will help you get back in tune with your body. You will become aware of the messages she is sending you. It will slow you down to the rhythm of God. It will help you to remove excess, get grounded, and purge you of the symptoms of disease. Relax into it. Do not reduce it to compulsion or some ritual of dissatisfaction. Allow yourself to be breathed by God.

Prostration will focus and ground you. After you release yourself, take heed of additional advice that will further assist you in managing stress.

Spiritual Stress Releasers

Enlist Your Husband's Support

You must allow your husband to understand that you have become overwhelmed by the level of stress in your life. I know he is busy and has a lot on him. But you are in this marriage together.

Neither of you should feel that you are alone. You must cherish one another so much that you know intuitively when the other is in pain. Intuition failing, open your mouth and say, "I am hurting. I need your support."

Honor Your Temple

The Scriptures teach that your body is the temple, the sanctuary of the Spirit of God. We have a treasure in these earthen vessels, which is the power of God (see 2 Corinthians 4:7). Therefore, honor your body through rest, nourishment, cleaning, and creative movement. Daily laughter can eliminate toxins from your body and spirit. Therefore, laugh well and laugh often. Learn once again to relax into your sexual passion.

Make New Friends

It is so much easier to navigate the waters of life when you have friends who go alongside you. Suffering is abated, sickness relieved, tragedy disarmed when you are in the presence of your friends. Renew old friendships, or seek out new ones. Be cautious not to engage friends who will enable your stressful habits. A true friend is not a reflection of our own image. Friends complement and supplement us. Yet, they are not parasitic, envious, or competitive. Pray that God will send you a friend after God's own heart, a friendship in which God is glorified. Then, be open and discerning so you will know when that friend appears. God knows the relationship that will resonate with your soul.

> Some friends play at friendship
>   but a true friend sticks closer than one's nearest kin.
>   —Proverbs 18:24 (NRSV)

Lighten Up!

You take being first lady quite seriously, just as you do every other task you undertake. It is serious business, for sure, because you are key in helping to point souls to the light. But, you must lighten up. Loosen up. Relax into your own creative style of leadership. Discover what works for you. Most of all, be flexible. Don't get stuck in thinking that your way is the only way of doing anything. And remember you don't have to do everything! Learn to say no. Delegate tasks to qualified, talented, and equipped saints.

Renew Your Style

Corporate chic may necessitate black, navy blue, or gray, but this is not the case in the black church. Brighten your wardrobe with colors such as fuchsia, orange, pink, turquoise, gold, and emerald. You have paid homage to your inner matron long enough. It's time to let your diva shine! Every woman has a unique body type, denominational culture, background, and experiences. Some women are naturally glamorous even in a t-shirt, jeans, and sandals. Others shine in ethnic or radically eclectic attire. We must enjoy the gift of our presence on the planet, honor the reflection in our own mirror, and work with what we got! Be at home in your own body. How you look should exude openness, confidence, and affirmation, never anxiety.

> But my dove, my perfect one, is unique,
>   the only daughter of her mother,
>   the favorite of the one who bore her.
> The maidens saw her and called her blessed;
>   the queens and concubines praised her.
>   —Song of Solomon 6:9 (NIV)

Dear one, you have nothing to prove. As an oblate, you can live a God-breathed life, a life that radiates divine love and compassion and a life that overflows with joy. "First lady" is not a death sentence. Your life is a sacred covenant trust to be lived to the glory of God. This does not diminish your uniqueness, intelligence, or independence. It simply references the spiritual magnitude of your marriage. Knowing this, may you drink from the cup of your mortality in peace and grace.

> I am still not all I should be, but I am focusing all my energies on this one thing: Forgetting the past, and looking forward to what lies ahead. (Philippians 3:13, NLT)

Covenant clergy marriage is in a perpetual state of transformation. As you grow, you learn more and more about God and about one another. You soon learn that it is not as much a matter of getting everything right as it is a relationship of dynamic self-discovery. We learn from our mess as well as our miracles! As you dismantle a lifestyle of stress, know that miracles will abound. Moreover, I am confident that both of you will be fine. Because, as you minister to others in the afterglow of your covenant love, your congregational life will be experienced as a blessing to be shared rather than a burden to be carried. And so it is that the woman who lives her life as an oblate is a woman of destiny.

Shekinah

Parenting

Jesus said, "Let the children come to me. Don't stop them!
For the Kingdom of Heaven belongs to such as these."
(Matthew 19:14, NLT)

Dear Shekinah,

Heaven loves children; their laughter is God's springtime. Children bring love, innocence, and an element of chaos that makes life interesting. Yes, children are a blessing. And, as they bless us, we must bless them with our consistent attention and constant energy.

Parenting is the most demanding position one can hold in life. Parenting in the spotlight of the parsonage can be especially challenging. While expectations of our children tend to be high, the demands of ministry often carry us away from our families. As a result, in busy clergy families, some children become wards of indulgence who are neither disciplined nor discipled. Some are even left unattended by the clergy parent.

Parenting is not an exact science. Childrearing tactics that may work with one child may have no impact on another, even within the same family. Therefore, we must be attuned to the special nuances of each child's personality. We must make each child aware that he or she is the image of God in the earth. We must teach them God's plan for salvation, to love and respect their bodies, and to demand that others do the same. Our role as parents is akin to a gardener's. Children reap what we sow into them. We must sow good things and good people into their lives.

We must also ensure that our children are well-rounded. At an early age, your children need to develop critical thinking skills, learn about their culture and heritage, learn a sport or musical instrument, or engage in other extracurricular endeavors. These are fundamental to full personhood. Be careful not to allow these extras and all the other mundane tasks of home, church, and school life to result in the overscheduling of your children's lives or your life, for that matter. Allow them some down time. Design a schedule that does not rob your little ones of their childhood.

Train up a child in the way he should go,
And when he is old he will not depart from it.
—*Proverbs 22:6 (NKJV)*

Spiritual Formation and Children

In all your giving, you must give your children a foundation through which they can build a strong faith in Jesus. In Lorraine Hansberry's play, *A Raisin in the Sun*, Lena Younger, the family's matriarch, announces in a powerful scene, "In this house there is God." Let this be your guiding mantra as you engage your children in spiritual formation. The following steps will assist you to create a Christ-like atmosphere for your children.

Create an Altar

Assist each child to create an altar to the Lord in his or her bedroom. It can be on a window sill, a tray, a small table, a cushion, a pillow, or a chair. Maintain a children's Bible there, and decorate the altar with a collage of Christian symbols and words. Affirm their sacred space by kneeling with them there to pray.

Encourage your children to pray for family, friends, and children around the world.

Teach Your Children the Tenets of the Faith

You and your husband must embrace the tenets of the faith and teach them to your children. These may include the Lord's Prayer, the Apostles' Creed, the Decalogue, the books of the Bible, and the prayer of salvation. Also, teach them the meaning of the sacraments, the liturgical calendar, and the importance of tithing and meeting the needs of others. A child's evangelism should begin in the home, where he or she shares in the ministry of hospitality, intercession, and benevolence. The fruit of this upbringing will be children who have moral clarity, personal integrity, and strength of character.

Be a Good Example

It is a vitally important that you live before your children as those who are redeemed of the Lord. Reflect Christ in your speech, temperament, actions, and relationships. Be aware of everything you say in your children's presence. Think about the possible impact of your words before you speak them. Above all, behave lovingly toward one another.

If you follow these three steps, you will have the makings of a family after God's own heart: a family who worships in spirit and truth; a family who manifests God's glory; a family who turns the heart of unbelievers to Jesus. A covenant marriage creates a covenant family who orders each day based on God's authority. You will "prosper and be in health, just as your soul prospers" (3 John 2, NKJV). When your communication is "as unto the Lord," tensions dissolve and reconciliation is perpetual. Yours will be a household for whom the joy of the Lord is strong and refreshing. The human enterprise will still include traffic, schoolyard skirmishes, bad hair days, and pouting. Nevertheless, God.

God is strong and can help you not to fall. He can bring you before his glory without any wrong in you and can give you great joy. (Jude 24, NCV)

Because you are the "primary" parent, you too must lay claim to seasons of refreshing and renewal.

Embracing the Gift of Solitude

As you raise your children in the fear and admonition of the Lord, do not neglect your own need for faith formation. To avoid being burnt out or overcome by exhaustion, I suggest you embrace the spiritual discipline of solitude. Although it may seem impossible, take a minimum of thirty minutes per day or three sessions of ten minutes per day to be alone with God. As much as possible, eliminate any source of distraction or external stimulation. Just close your eyes as you visualize yourself seated before the throne of God.

Allow the light of the throne room to penetrate every cell of your body. Experience the beauty of the Light as it breathes healing and rest into your soul. Bathe your thoughts in the serenity of this realm. Drink deeply of God's peace. And, know that you are a vessel of Light, of the most high God.

Remain in total awareness of the divine presence. Liberated by solitude, exult in the name of the Lord.

As you sit, let this be your continuous inward command: "Be still, and know that I am God." Stillness for a parent can be a defiant act of faith. Stillness is not only physical, but a spiritual state. Finding time for physical stillness, given your family's busy schedules, can be a seemingly insurmountable challenge. Yet, if your household is going to operate effectively, you must find some still time. And, through your stillness, your knowledge of God's presence will increase. Through the power of God's presence, you will cry out as Thomas did when he discovered he was in the presence of the risen Savior, "My Lord and my God!" (John 20:28, NCV). And, like Thomas, you will no doubt receive the peace of God.

As you practice solitude, God will bless your life with many gifts: simplicity, silence, inner spaciousness, awareness, illumination, and wisdom. Solitude refreshes the soul, brings balance, and will prepare your heart for whatever lies ahead. Through the power of the Holy Spirit, you will create your own rhythm of engagement, your own vocabulary and connection. These will become evident as you increase your ability to emotionally disconnect from frivolous thought, anxiety-provoking memories, and the need to be in control. Listen well to your body. Honor your feelings. Create healthy boundaries that will allow you to protect your personal time and space.

"Whenever you pray, go into your room and shut the door and pray to your Father who is in secret."
(Matthew 6:6, NRSV)

Your husband and children need to understand when it is Momma's time. Your place of solitude can be your bathtub or in your parked car during the thirty minutes before the children finish their school day. A bench in a museum, park, or mall, or even an empty sanctuary can serve as a place of solitude. Wherever and whenever you decide to practice solitude, be present in the moment with God, and God will commune with you. Note, however, that to receive its full benefits, you must practice solitude when you are not so tired that you lack the energy to be fully present. With practice, your ability to be still in the presence of the Lord will increase.

In quietness and in trust shall be your strength.
(Isaiah 30:15, NRSV)

Solitude and Covenant Vows

To some it would seem an innate impossibility to be both married and solitary. Yet some solitude, even from your spouse, is necessary for a healthy covenant marriage, especially where children are involved. There may even be times when you and your spouse will need to abstain sexually from each other. Such abstinence must be practiced with total prayer and consecration and, most important, mutual consent.

Every mother needs personal time and space to refuel, reflect, re-create, and be inspired. Your husband likely has many scheduled getaways such as conferences, retreats, board meetings, lectures, revivals, and preaching engagements, all of which provide time for adult conversation, restaurant dining, and hotel maid service. You need time to be childless and care-free, too! Therefore, ask your husband to help facilitate some getaway time for you. Solitude must become a lifestyle, not simply an emergency reaction.

As you are revived and refueled, you will become increasingly at home in your own spirit. You will be able to impart confidence and joy to your children. Your discernment will escalate. A woman who does not fear her own solitude is a woman whom God can trust with dreams and visions, for she is not shamed by her nakedness or diminished by humility. Her soul is spacious, her capacity for good unblemished. She wears the rainbow and the sky.

When solitude has ended, the world seems a noisome place, brash, unthinking, insensitive. But remain centered. Be slow to speak and eager to listen. Breathe deeply. Walk gracefully. Sing a new song. Shimmer. Be the peace. Exhale beatitudes. Open your heart.

Mothering Wisely

Motherhood is a parable of the Crucifixion. Both demand unconditional, unwavering, and suffering love. Both exact physical pain and the shedding of blood that new life must come forth. The labor, the passion is absolute. So is the hope and the expected glory. Yet, out of you came forth not just a physical likeness but a living soul. The prayer of every covenant mother is that her child will become everything that Jesus died for that child to be! And we live our lives to usher them into their divine destiny. We pray that our lives will be a bridge and not a detour, a stepping stone rather than a road block. We pray that we will give them wings for flying, the courage to dream, and the faith to endure adversity.

Motherhood is honorable and to be honored. Being a full-time mother does not make you less than professional or competent or informed or sophisticated. In this millennium, mothering is a courageous act of devotion. It is an interdisciplinary wonder—pediatrician, educator, psychologist, nutritionist, evangelist, financial analyst, community organizer, public relations professional, volunteer, full-time maintenance staff, comedian, teacher's aide, referee, and friend. Take a bow! Raise your own flag! Wear a button that says "applause." Stand strong. Your labor is not in vain.

Always give yourselves fully to the work of the Lord.
You know that your work in the Lord is never wasted.
(1 Corinthians 15:58, NCV)

Mothers are not infallible. Never presume to be. You come to this holy office with a very real past, as well as some not very easily-disguised issues. Relate to your children in ways that you will be attuned to their needs, their fears, their interests, and their joys. Tap into the skills and resources of your pediatrician, teacher, and play mothers to maximize your parenting.

Do not force your child to carry the burden of your self-esteem or social ambition. Bestow upon your dear ones the blessings of a sacred childhood. That child is blessed who knows that she or he is loved, safe, appreciated, and included.

Finally, let wisdom by your gatekeeper. Wisdom's daughters are alone with God in the dark places of life. In solitude, you will discover that wisdom is a tree of life, a bed to sleep in, a source of beauty. Light shines from wisdom leading us to the way of God. Wisdom's desire for the future motivates the wise woman to choose humility over fame, favor over success, compassion over power, and service over recognition.

In solitude, the wise woman moves her prayers in solidarity with every just cause to bring peace on earth, reclaim hope for the oppressed, cleanse the world of disease, and redeem humanity for the worship and service of the Lord. Her legacy is peace, resilience, and grace. Her "children rise up and call her blessed" (Proverbs 31:28, NKJV).

Parenting Adult Children

Wisdom is the most important thing. So get wisdom.
If it costs everything you have, get understanding.
Believe in the value of wisdom, and it will make you great.
Use it, and it will bring honor to you.
Like flowers in your hair, it will beautify your life.
Like a beautiful crown, it will make you look
beautiful.
—*Proverbs 4:7-9 (NCV)*

It is a recipe for disaster to attempt to parent adult children in the same way that we parent minor children. The same forces—the world, the culture, and the devil—actively work to corrupt and spoil family life. Yet even clergy parents soon learn that it is far easier to bring healing when a child has bruised a knee than when that child in adulthood bruises career, marriage, integrity, or finances.

So much of the stress we experience when parenting adult children is rooted in watching them live through the consequences of bad decisions and maintaining a posture that keeps us from getting in the way of what God wants to do in their lives. Only the wisdom of God gives us power to withstand every assault of confusion and destruction.

"For this reason, I bow my knees before the Father,
from whom every family in heaven and on earth takes
its name." (Ephesians 3:14-15, NRSV)

Righteousness is not achieved by way of inheritance. Nor will material indulgence establish the faith, maturity, integrity, or happiness of the adult child. Bishop John and I would like to share some practices that we hope will provide affirmation, relief, and encouragement to clergy parents of adult children.

1. Affirm your unconditional love.
2. Counsel without "ruling."
3. Do not live your life through them.

4. Respect them as adults.
5. Respect their parenting styles and values.
6. Do not promote a relationship of dependence—emotional, financial, or social.
7. Insist on respect for your time, your space, your priorities, and your needs.
8. Do not interfere in their marriage unless invited.
9. Do not draw them into your arguments.
10. Become their greatest intercessors!

"And in your descendents all the families of the earth shall be blessed." (Acts 3:25, NRSV)

LETTER 9

Financial Stress

My God, my God, why have you forsaken me?
  Why are you so far from saving me,
  so far from the words of my groaning?
—Psalm 22:1 (NIV)

Ah, Megiddo,

Covenant clergy marriage offers incredible blessings. But when the pastor divorces the first lady and their shared home is the parsonage of the church, the wife and her minor children find themselves in the wilderness. It provokes a Hagar state of mind that can bring desperation.

On your wedding night, you did not dream that you would suffer a humiliating descent from first lady to emotional purgatory, nor did you expect to take your children with you. Yes, you have been dealt a terrible blow that is exacerbated by the pariah treatment by the church leaders. You are greeted tepidly by the sisters in the supermarket. How did the adulterer-abuser get to be the victim, you may ask yourself. I, too, am clueless. Where are all the souls you led to Christ, counseled by prayer, and tutored in the gospel? Ask Jesus on Calvary.

A front-row seat at the battle for your soul between good and evil will surely paralyze you if you allow it to become the focus of your consciousness. My counsel? Hide your heart in the palace of worship. Do not to be lured away by fear, revenge, anxiety, frustration, or any other debilitating spirit. As difficult as it may be, weep, but don't wallow! "Be angry, and do not sin" (Ephesians 4:26, NKJV). Remember, no matter what it looks like right now, "God is not unjust; he will not forget your work and the love that you have shown him as you have helped his people and continue to help them" (Hebrews 6:10, NIV). Your husband may have abandoned you, taking his flock with him, but remember that God is "with you always" (Matthew 28:20, NIV). As with Hagar, God's favor upon you and your children cannot be aborted.

First Things First

Your first order of business must be to assure that you and your children have enough resources on which to live. Socioeconomic data indicate that when families divorce, the standard of living for women and children decreases while that of men increases. Facing the cold shoulder of immediate and immense poverty can be more than disheartening. However, do not develop the mentality that you are trapped. Rather, consider yourself in transition, that sacred ground between promise and fulfillment.

This transitional period will help you explore and tap into the power of your underutilized gifts and talents. Consider all the skills that you have used voluntarily in the church and the community—organizing events, providing elder and child care, coalition building, fundraising, hospitality, political advocacy, parenting education, and counseling. These marketable skills have the potential to open fresh streams of income for you and your children. Do not accept the notion that your gifts are not worthy of pay, simply because you used them voluntarily in the church. You may even chart your own path as an entrepreneur. In the short run, however, you need salaried employment. Your first job may not provide you and your children with an income to support the lifestyle to which you are accustomed. But understand that wherever necessity places you at this time is not your destiny!

It is important that you explain to your children that they, too, are in transition. This would be a good time to explain to them the difference between wants and needs. They need to understand that they will have to forego the bling bling that many of their peers have. You and they will learn that God will meet you at the point of your need. Three times in the Gospel of Matthew, the Lord says to you and your children, "Do not worry" (Matthew 6:25-27, 31-32, 34, NIV). Remember, too, the angel of the Lord responded to the cry of Hagar's child (see Genesis 21:17).

With respect to your children's educational needs, private school is not a necessity. Many successful people are products of public schools. They succeeded because education was a family value. Your children are not doomed to be thugs, social parasites, or victims of violence in the hood just because they attend public schools.

This is your season to learn about money. What attracts it, makes it grow, and allows it to stand firm? When is it available? What deters it? The assistance of a financial planner may be useful as you process this worldly matter. You must also learn about prosperity and abundance from God's perspective. What is the relationship between dominion and abundance? How do you qualify for supernatural success? In the next chapter of your life, intend that you will not simply survive but will penetrate the zone of "exceedingly abundantly above all that we ask or think" (Ephesians 3:20, KJV). Debt, dependence, and desperation will come to an end.

Worship Invokes the Light

While you are addressing the worldly matters that are essential to your family's survival, you must seek and stay in the presence of God. You are beset by darkness of the highest magnitude that can suck the life out of one who is not God-breathed. Nothing can shatter this darkness except prayer and undefiled worship. Worship will keep you in the presence of God. For "in [God's] presence there is fullness of joy" (Psalm 16:11, NRSV). Worship will keep you connected to the Source, the Provider.

In this present state of abject need, how can you be needless before the throne of God? Will you bring your tithe when all you have is monetary scraps from a now distant lover? You can, and you must. For true worship demands of the soul what making love demands of the body—passion, single-mindedness, and complete surrender.

"You shall worship the LORD *your God,*
And I will bless your bread and your water;
And I will take sickness away from among you."
—*Exodus 23:25* (NRSV)

When your heart is immersed in the worship of the Lord, no evil thing can approach it. Even as you struggle to make ends meet, through worship you must allow yourself to become disconnected from the seductive power of money. This will require supernatural intervention! When bills are due, when "baby needs a new pair of shoes," it is difficult not to focus on lack of money. But know that the angel of the Lord goes before you to provide safe passage through this wilderness. This is not superstition or hocus-pocus. Rather, it is a love supreme.

The path that leads to true worship is the path of self-denial. Your flesh may inquire, "What further denial can there be than for a covenant wife to be forsaken by her spouse, humiliated in the church, and debased in front of her children?" As difficult as it may be, keep Calvary ever before you as you worship! Visions of Calvary have the power to soften the heart and refresh our faith.

You see, worship is a decision of the heart, a personal act of volition, a faith response to grace, an occasion of love freely given, and an oblation of the soul. Worship is invoked by the character of God. The essence of the Divine becomes alive to our consciousness and awakens in us the desire to worship. In that moment, self must relinquish any claim it has whether for bread, encouragement, even life. God is all. All is God.

The light of God never shines brighter than in the soul of one who worships "in spirit and truth" (John 4:23, NIV). There is glory in this shining of unblemished holiness and supernatural love. It is surely a mystery that, having been wounded by love, you can only be healed by loving. Undistracted by the past, unintimidated by the future, allow your soul to erupt in a holocaust of love for our sovereign, omnipotent, and merciful God.

This is true worship:

Boundless adoration

An uninterrupted crescendo of beatitude.

A reverential flood of wordless awe!

Ordination does not assure it, nor can protocol restrain it.

Worship creates a tabernacle of light so extreme that even good people behold themselves as filthy rags in its fire. Your confidence, aspirations, and peace of mind will be healed in the miracle of worship. Soon it will be your turn to shine! Take your bow and walk in radiant serenity. You will be a lady first in integrity, first in resilience, and first in grace. In time, worship will be your bread and your water.

Therefore, since we are receiving a kingdom that cannot be shaken, let us give thanks, by which we offer to God an acceptable worship with reverence and awe. (Hebrews 12:28, NRSV)

Seven Keys to Worship

I have discovered seven keys to a fresh understanding of worship. Each leads to the unfolding of multiple dimensions of revelation. It is possible that you will experience everything from a theophany to unrelenting weeping to a surge of apocalyptic fire in the depths of your soul. Do not seek after or desire or resist any of the above. Only, openly and fully worship the Lord our God. Free yourself of everything you thought you knew about worship. Pray the Holy Spirit to aid, inspire, teach, and guide you into true worship. The keys are not rules. Instead, they are fragments from revelation and experience. They are not flawless but certainly helpful.

Worship God! (Revelation 22:9, NRSV)

- True worship is not merely an occasion or event; it is the unbroken exaltation of the Lord in the heart of the redeemed.

- True worship can be either audible or wordless.
- True worship creates sanctuary.
- True worship manifests the glory of God.
- True worship is warfare between light and darkness.
- True worship changes the atmosphere on earth.
- The soul ablaze in worship never dies.

Fear God, and give glory to him; . . . worship him that made heaven, and earth, and the sea, and the fountains of waters. (Revelation 14:7, KJV)

A woman in worship becomes a vessel endued with supernatural grace, insight, and resilience. She rises to her highest self when she humbles herself in worship. In this season, more than any other, being a true worshipper will establish you and ground you and conform you to your prophetic purpose. You and your seed will enjoy the abundant life. Worship is a soul journey of ascent into the depths of God. Paul states, "We . . . beholding as in a glass the glory of the Lord, are changed into the same image from glory to glory, even as by the Spirit of the Lord" (2 Corinthians 3:7, KJV).

Poverty is real. Lack is tangible. Credit scores have power. You have been divorced by the man you love. But you are not defeated. You are transitioning to another realm of glory "by the Spirit of the Lord." One day at a time you will begin to shape a new life. Remember this—your destiny remains unchanged! You are still God's woman. This is not the path that you have chosen. Worship anyway. Your dreams appear to be on hold. Worship anyway. Your daily battle is with the spirit of humiliation and anger. Worship anyway. You have no money! Worship anyway!

The LORD will guide you continually,
and satisfy your needs in parched places,
and make your bones strong.
—Isaiah 58:11 (NRSV)

I have known poverty,
smelled its breath when other children were tantalized
by the aroma of baked cookies and warm bread.

I have been more than touched by poverty;
I have been raped by its indifference, isolated by its
    classism, and mocked by its guardians.
I have tasted poverty around the world—Africa, India,
    the isles of the sea.
It is bitter, poisonous, filthy.
Swallowing up infants and elderly with a gulp.
Reducing strong men to beggars.
Creating a whoredom of an entire generation.
Those who are found by God in their poverty are
    the true saints.
And those who minister to the poor, the real angels.
Do not give poverty your mind. Nor let it penetrate
    your soul.
You have been created for life!

It is the time for you to call God by name,
by the name that opens rivers of revelation for you
    and your children:
Jehovah Shammah. It means "The LORD is There"
    (Ezekiel 48:35, NRSV).
Jehovah Shammah,
My thoughts embrace you.
I trace your form with weeping doxologies.
You alone silence the pangs of my longing.
Your glory creates a tabernacle for my hope.
Your right arm is a fortress between me and desperation.
I shall not want.
My "daily bread" is always fresh.
You wait with me on every line of humiliation.
You give me the words for every bureaucratic form.
You shake the weariness from my soul.
You raise up strangers to bless us.
Thank you!

Creating a God-breathed Life

While pursuing a God-breathed life, you will come to understand what it means to be in the world but not of the world.

◆

With the power of the Holy Spirit, turn the volume down on
  ego-centered thinking.
In an atmosphere of confrontation, be the love of God.
Daily explore and expand your opportunities for generosity.
  "A generous [woman] will prosper, [she] who refreshes others
  will [herself] be refreshed" (Proverb 11:25, NIV).
Coach yourself to be harmless toward others.
Be the blessing in the world.
Consume less.
Maintain a posture of intercession.
Forgive.
Honor your creative impulse.
Because Christ is in you—
Shine.

*God heard the boy crying. And God's angel called to
Hagar from heaven. He said, "What is wrong, Hagar?
Don't be afraid! God has heard the boy crying there.
Help the boy up. Take him by the hand. I will make his
descendants into a great nation." (Genesis 21:17-18,
NCV)*

Megiddo, in this wilderness of transition, you are not an after-thought. You and your children are very much on God's mind and heart. Allow the Spirit of the Lord to breathe strength, courage, and wisdom into your life. Let your worship be your warfare! Let your worship bring you sanctuary! Let your worship transform your atmosphere from lack to abundance, rejection to inclusion, dependence to freedom, sadness to joy, great joy! "I pray that you may prosper in all things and be in health, just as your soul prospers" (3 John 2, NKJV).

LETTER 10

Adultery with a Woman

Let marriage be held in honor by all,
and let the marriage bed be kept undefiled.
(Hebrews 13:4, NRSV)

Dear Emmaus,

Covenant clergy marriage is a vow to advance the mystery of the gospel in the earth. It is a system for recycling the compassion and forgiveness of God into human experience. It is elastic yet firm. It changes us without itself being changed. It sets a standard for intimacy that must be held inviolate. Through it, the healing of the Lord can be experienced. By it, the voice of God descends into the natural corridors of our lives. When covenant clergy marriage is good, it is very good. But when it is bad, it is vile. You have experienced the vilest of assaults to any marriage, most especially covenant clergy marriage: betrayal through adultery.

Adultery torments the soul. It tears at the heart, brutally unraveling the mind. You know this all too well. You responded to your husband's first incident of infidelity with grace, compassion, and forgiveness. Regrettably, a pattern has emerged, and your marriage has become a roller-coaster ride between bliss and purgatory. His rituals of repentance have grown more and more extravagant, suggesting that he is aware of the magnitude of his betrayal. Yet he continues to live a life out of control. Not only has your marriage suffered, but also the integrity of your husband's ministry has been severely compromised.

After each act of infidelity, you pray, hope, want to believe in him, only to be disappointed. You are in a difficult place. Authentic covenant marriage must contain bonds of trust, holiness, and mutual compassion. All of these are missing in your marriage. To make matters worse, your husband has woven a web of denial, making it virtually impossible to get to the root of the real problem. Wanting to protect your marriage and your family at any cost, you have engaged in a level of denial of your own.

Your faith may make you reluctant to divorce. It is not my role to question or condemn your faith; however, I will say this: The covenant does not require that you sacrifice your sanity, your health, or your salvation. If there comes a point when you believe any of these are in jeopardy, gather your courage and walk to safety. Adultery is a form of abuse. By its nature, if abuse is tolerated, it tends to escalate. Shame and humiliation can torment. They have the power to deteriorate your self-value, self-respect, and mental health. Through it all, remember, it's not your fault! There's nothing wrong with you! Adultery is the adulterer's decision.

I believe firmly that effectual intercession can triumph over the forces of evil. I also know that lust, pride, and volition can wage a mighty resistance. Your soul is at war in the most vulnerable areas of your life. Even when the warfare has ended, you will have to be just as diligent about engaging in the process that leads to the healing and restoration of your marriage. Be careful not to lose yourself along the way.

Only you know the path by which the Lord is leading you. As you prayerfully consider God's will for your marriage, I recommend a spiritual discipline that will provide ongoing relief and encouragement. Whether or not the Spirit leads you to remain in your marriage, remain in constant intercession for your husband. Pray that his heart will turn back to you and God. My heart's desire in Christ Jesus is that your marriage be restored, that the Lord will not give him over to a reprobate mind, that an overwhelming conviction of sin comes quickly followed by repentance to God. For any sin against marriage is a sin against God. I am praying, therefore, with you that his heart returns to God.

The Spiritual Discipline of Self-Care

The prophet Hosea prayed to return the heart of the transgressor to the Lord. If your marriage and the ministry are to survive, that must also be your prayer. You cannot endure such a calling on your own strength. Therefore, I encourage you to pursue a discipline of self-care. Through this discipline, you can maintain a sense of balance and inner peace.

Self-care has both a practical and spiritual dimension. Chief among the practical concerns is that your husband's infidelity has exposed you to the possibility of contracting sexually transmitted diseases, the most deadly of which is HIV/AIDS. You must get tested for HIV/AIDS and insist that your husband do the same. Furthermore, it is urgent that you use a condom whenever you have sexual intercourse with him. You cannot put yourself at risk of death because of your husband's repeated indiscretions. Be adamant and unrelenting in this regard. Your life depends upon you standing strong. Personal counseling will help you navigate this season of your life.

I recommend the following practical methods of self-care:

- Develop healthy relationships with persons outside of your congregation.
- Expand your circle of interest and opportunity.
- Honor your body with rest, nutrition, and exercise.
- Find a consistent source of inspiration and affirmation.
- Take steps to secure your financial future by completing your college education, securing gainful employment with benefits, eliminating all credit card debt, and finding out the current status of your insurance policies and other investments.

To pray is not a cop-out. Prayer strengthens resilience and will give you peace.

God's power has been working in us. We have righteousness as our weapon, both to attack and defend ourselves. (2 Corinthians 6:7, NLT)

The above will provide balance to your life so that you can fight for your marriage from a position of strength. Only you can decide what the office of first lady means to you in this hour. Do you stand as a bulwark? Or do you gracefully decline and absent yourself while you undergo marriage therapy? It may even be a Sunday-to-Sunday decision. Let your self-care process decide for you. Remember, psychological martyrdom is not part of the covenant.

Self-care begins with self-love: to love your soul, your life, your body, your gifts, your personality, your dreams. Self-love has the power to cast out fear. Self-care has as one of its privileges to teach others how to love and respect us. Self-care establishes our borders and protects our sacred ground. Queen Vashti is a holy exemplar of self-care. She is a reminder of our own royal status.

The sting of adultery penetrates through the very bone and marrow of a woman's self-esteem. It is soul crushing. It is a death blow like no other. Consequently, self-care is tantamount to resurrection. Can this woman live again? It's a process. And, three days do not provide nearly enough time. For the betrayed spouse, every day is Good Friday—pain, darkness, and loss.

From the treasure of my own healing, I bring you gifts, the simplicity of which may initially disappoint you. Nevertheless, simplicity is the perfect antidote for chaos. Call upon either of these gifts at any time for as long as you require.

There are times when it is too difficult to find God. When we are confined, it feels as though the world is closing in on us. We need to break out. This is one of those times. Your faith formation will be enriched and your emotions blessed if you undertake peripatetic (walking) meditation. I am confident that it will provide multiple benefits at a time when your mind is racing and you are battling insomnia and emotional fatigue. I am also aware that you're finding it difficult to pray.

The Discipline of Walking Meditation

Even when I walk
through the dark valley of death,
I will not be afraid,
for you are close beside me.
Your rod and your staff
protect and comfort me.
—Psalm 23:4 (NLT)

There is a powerful connection between mind, body, and soul. What affects one area is experienced in the others, positively and negatively. Exercising helps the body release endorphins, which eliminate stress and anxiety, thereby creating a sense of calm and well-being. Therefore, I bestow upon you the gift of walking meditation. Step into your radiance as you ponder God's love for you. You are "fearfully and wonderfully made." Give thanks and rejoice.

A walking meditation will greatly benefit you. You are consumed with sadness and feelings of rejection. You are tied up in knots emotionally and perhaps physically. You may have forgotten how to let go and trust. Walking with God will enable you to breathe again. As you engage in walking meditation, I encourage you to focus on five words that I believe have the power to begin healing your inner life. They are breathe, movement, beauty, passion, and song.

Breathe

Then he breathed on them and said to them, "Receive the Holy Spirit." (John 20:22, NLT)

You are a Spirit woman. This is your divine nature, your compass, and your guide. You have received the breath of God. You have entered the royal priesthood. Breath is glory.

Breathe is the word of awakening, opening, receiving, and releasing. It is the word that proclaims life and imbues us with the Spirit of the Lord. This word is given to remind you that so long as there is breath, there is life. There is life for yourself, even life for your marriage. Most of all, there is abundant life in Jesus Christ. Remember to breathe. Breathe freely. Breathe fully and be refreshed.

Movement

Jesus said to the people, "I am the light of the world. If you follow me, you won't be stumbling through the darkness, because you will have the light that leads to life." (John 8:12, NLT)

Very often we are paralyzed by our pain. Unable to move. Yet movement brings vitality and authority. It penetrates every cell, every organ, every muscle and system in your body, and it has the power to dislodge heaviness from your spirit. This word is given to remind you to keep going! Becoming stagnant is not an option. God has much for you to do, much for you to contribute to the kingdom. Much for you to discover and recover. Get yourself up!

Beauty

Pain covers our lives with a veil. We are unable to see beyond our own suffering. Courage removes the veil.

Honor and majesty are before Him;
Strength and beauty are in His sanctuary.
—Psalm 96:6 *(NKJV)*

Take this word. Allow it to open your eyes and your heart. Write it across your mirror and in the palm of your hand.

Beauty is a creative word. It brings awareness, mystery, and grace. This word activates the fertile field of the imagination. Without beauty, remorse, unforgiveness, and bitterness can forever sabotage your joy. Remember your beauty. Your husband's betrayal cannot diminish the beauty that God has placed inside you. Let beauty surround you, embrace you, and nourish you.

Passion

This is the fire that makes woman whole. It is the power that cannot be denied. It is the word for a soul being tried.

*"When you go through deep waters and great trouble,
I will be with you. When you go through rivers of
difficulty, you will not drown! When you walk through
the fire of oppression, you will not be burned up; the
flames will not consume you." (Isaiah 43:2, NLT)*

You are your passion. Passion engineers purpose and makes destiny certain. Your passion is your integrity. Hold on to it.

Passion is the word of all-consuming covenant love. It is love that bends but does not break. This word will go before you to create "springs in the desert" (Isaiah 43:20). Without passion, life is a hopeless, dreamless, nothing. Through all of this, remain passionate about your life and your future. Remember that you are lovable and loving, that you bear in your body the covenant and vision of the most high God. Wear this word like a badge upon your heart.

Song

There is a certain magic in song. No one really understands why it has the power that it does.

*When the LORD restored his exiles to Jerusalem
  it was like a dream!
We were filled with laughter,
  and we sang for joy.
—Psalm 126:1-2 (NLT)*

Unleash the song in your belly. Write the lyrics that will make you whole. Choose a melody that soothes and completes you.

Song is the word of God's favor. It is the word of triumph and victory over all the works of evil. Song is a gift from eternity. Song bursts from the womb of your soul completely engaged in a crescendo of glory. Keep a song in your heart. Let melodies of hope and love resonate within your being. The fifth word is the word that contains all the others.

The fifth word ushers in the supernatural, opens the gates of the city, and erases dark clouds. This is the word of new beginnings. It is the word of all words. It is the word that sparked creation. It cannot be defined, silenced, or killed. This word is the word of life. Drink deeply of it and be renewed.

The Process of Walking Meditation

On the glorious splendor of your majesty,
and on your wondrous works, I will meditate.
(Psalm 145:5, NRSV)

Meditate on these words as you walk: breathe, movement, beauty, passion, song. Allow each word to penetrate your inner core. They are your words that spring from the character of God. Repeat your words with clarity, acceptance, and humility. Enunciate them in deep contemplation. Wrap your thoughts and your heart around your words. Deposit them in the bank of your soul's longing. Speak these words inwardly with intention and faith. Allow each word to become a matter of the heart. Sow them into your thoughts, allowing them to take root in your mind, heart, and spirit.

As you walk, be aware of your surroundings and begin to bathe your soul in thanksgiving. Thank God for all that your eyes see, for what your ears hear, and for what you smell or touch. Thank God for the activity of your limbs. The breath of life in your body. The movement of the universe is your movement. The beauty of the earth is the beauty within you. The passion of Calvary is your passion. The song of creation is your song.

Walk in the light of restoration. Walk until the Word you carry begins to carry you. Breathe the sacred breath. Allow your tears to flow like healing streams of mercy. Walk through the gates of praise. Walk with your heart on tiptoe. Walk from the depths of your being. Walk into revelation. Walk with a child's heart. Walk until your soul is embraced by silence. As you walk, rest in your words.

I leave you with this word of assurance. You do not walk alone. You walk with God, in whom all possibilities exist. Your five miracle words are drawn from the character of God. Speak them well. Speak them strong. Unleash your sacred power in the eternal light of God's love. Through these words, know that the healing of the Lord has begun.

Daughters of Zoar

Adultery with a Man

They shall not come near to me, to serve me as priest,
nor come near any of my sacred offerings, the things that are
most sacred; but they shall bear their shame, and the
consequences of the abominations that they have committed.
(Ezekiel 44:13, NRSV)

To the Daughters of Zoar,

How do you live with the realization that your husband is having
an affair with another man? Some of you have walked in as your
marriage bed was being defiled. Others have been deflecting
rumors until you were finally confronted with the reality of this
tormenting betrayal. Others of you have chosen to remain in the
marriage in spite of the ongoing shadow relationship. In your
silence, the shame, fear, and humiliation have nearly wrung the
life out of your souls. The suspicion, the jealousy, the shocking
confirmation, the rage, and the palpable hurt have consumed you.
You each recognize that you are a woman at risk, a woman at war,
a woman in need of supernatural intervention.

*"Who can bring a clean thing out of an unclean? No one
can." (Job 14:4, NRSV)*

Recently, there has been a great deal of discussion in the African American community about men who live on the down low. Numerous articles, talk shows, and publications have explored the lives of men who live publicly as heterosexuals yet have hidden away a life of active homosexuality. The impact of this phenomenon upon the wife, children, and ministry has been profoundly traumatic. While the down low concept is nothing new, in an age of HIV/AIDS, the potential consequences are more grave.

At this moment, I am sure you are not interested in any historical backdrop, psychological analyses, or sociological statistics. Rather, you want God to provide a means of escape. You want your life back. You want to maintain your dignity in the face of public humiliation and position yourself for healing. Yes, you want to live happily ever after. You want to know what to do

after being rebuked with "I thought you knew!"
after sitting martyr-style at the burial
after going to be tested for HIV/AIDS
after having his mother blame you
after the media circus goes away
after the church votes him out
after the children receive therapy
after he fasts to be delivered
after he promises you financial bliss to stay
after you "forgive and forget"

In the hour of your crisis, I encourage you to read the Book of Jude in its entirety. Lay hold of verses 20 and 21 in particular:

But you, beloved, build yourselves up on your most holy faith; pray in the Holy Spirit; keep yourselves in the love of God; look forward to the mercy of our Lord Jesus Christ that leads to eternal life. (NRSV)

When your husband is a man of the cloth, it is important that you do not interpret his sin as a failure on God's part. You must not direct your anger at God or at the church. The church didn't betray you; he did. Nor should you allow his partner to become the sole focus of your contempt. You have been violated and deceived only by your covenant spouse. Do not equate his love with God's love for you. It would be a heinous crime to give your husband the power to cause you to reject God. Nor should embarrassment run you out of the church. Change your membership, not your faith in Jesus Christ. The betrayal you have experienced has no easy consolation. Get all the support available to you. Get on with your life, knowing that the prayers of the saints are being uttered on your behalf. I have written this blessing especially for you.

And now,
May the love of God arouse you from your stupor,
Motivate you to embrace your inner diva,
Give you the courage to co-create with destiny a new life
of beauty, purpose, and celebration.
May you discover an inner source of serenity
in times of conflict.
May you be well in mind, body, and spirit.
May you accomplish great things in the majesty
of your faith.
May you know and own your kingdom value.
May you soon be cleansed of all hurt, shame,
and humiliation.
May you prosper.
May laughter be yours.
May all your dreams come true.
Amen.

LETTER 12

Arimathea

Sickness

Bless the LORD, O my soul,
  and do not forget all his benefits—
who forgives all your iniquity,
  who heals all your diseases.
  —Psalm 103:2-3 (NRSV)

Dear Arimathea,

My heart is touched by your infirmity. Because you are so accustomed to being superactive, I realize how difficult it must be for you to be bedridden. I am prayerful that your faith remains strong. The helplessness and anxiety created by sickness have the power to heighten the fear of the unknown, thereby challenging your faith. I also know that being away from the church can be difficult. While you may be tempted to run things from your sick bed, resist the urge; otherwise, you can corrupt the healing process. Don't worry. New leaders can and will emerge in your absence.

Because for you the ministry of the gospel is paramount, you are troubled by your current inability to serve. Remember that your covenant vows include sickness. "In sickness and in health" covers everything from the common cold to cancer to mental illness or any other debilitating condition. It is an unwavering promise of fidelity and care, twenty-four hours a day for as long as it takes, the loss of hair, faculties, mobility, or control of bodily functions notwithstanding. It is a love far greater than romantic feeling. It is the bonding of souls that creates covenant love.

When we marry, our expectation is eternal bliss. While we know that suffering is possible, we just don't believe it will befall us. When sickness arrives, it thwarts our naive expectations and floods our minds with a host of questions. How do I maintain my dignity? How do I preserve my sense of self? How do I "wife" when my body won't cooperate with me? How do I maintain a sense of God's favor? How will my condition affect my husband's perception of and response to me?

Pondering these and other questions can cause your imagination to run away with you, leading you into a forest of depression. Try not to go there! Rather, hope in God.

Hope must be your guide as you plow through this unknown territory. Hope is the intangible power that is freely imparted to us as disciples of our Lord Jesus Christ. The apostle Paul says we are prisoners of hope. Hope allows us to get excited about what we have not yet seen. Pregnancy teaches us to hope. Applying for the first home loan teaches us to hope. Sickness is yet another learning ground for hope to spring forth! Hope is the bridge between disease and recovery, debt and prosperity, enmity and reconciliation. In this hour, you are called by hope, nothing doubting. Let images of hope saturate your atmosphere with beauty, simplicity, and inspiration. Hope is the stuff that miracles are made of.

The Light of Intercession

In spite of your infirmity, you can engage in kingdom work. Give serious consideration to the discipline of intercession. Through intercession, you will refresh yourself as you refresh others. An intercessor strives to touch the heart of God with the hurt of humanity and to touch the hurt of humanity with the heart of God. Being an intercessor requires compassion and an understanding of the Word of God. Spending time alone with God is a given. More than anything, you must possess a willingness to lay your personal concerns aside. As an intercessor, you share in the resurrection work of Jesus Christ. You will come to know and experience personally the grace and gift of the delegated power of God! There is no greater calling.

The priestly prayer of Jesus found in John 17 is the consummate intercessory prayer. It makes for an appropriate starting point. As you embark on this journey of intercession, study this prayer. It will allow you to hear and learn the heart of God. As you pray this prayer, allow your soul to meld with Jesus. Try to commit to memory those verses that prick your heart.

To further aid in your practice, I offer you a weekly model of intercession to help you get started. You will need a Bible and a notebook to jot down thoughts and inspirations. Each day is guided by a prayer focus. Your intercessions will go out to individuals and those who suffer wherever they are in the world. As your prayers bring healing to others, you, too, will be healed. Intercession is a holy office. It should not be taken lightly. The power of your faith will have global impact. An abiding love for others is the only true motivation of an intercessor. She is one driven by compassion.

Monday: Peace on Earth

> *The LORD will settle international disputes. All the nations will beat their swords into plowshares and their spears into pruning hooks. All wars will stop. (Isaiah 2:4, NLT)*

Let this prophecy ignite your soul and ground your faith. You are about to co-labor with God. The world is in need of a proliferation of people who believe that peace is possible in our lifetime.

Guided by the words of Isaiah, use a pocket world atlas and information from news sources to identify and pray for continents, nations, and people groups who are experiencing conflict. Pray for peace. Pray for effectual diplomacy. Pray for political stability. Pray for leaders who have a vision for the uplift of humanity. Envision the hand of God moving upon the earth as light shattering darkness. Experience your prayers uniting peacemakers worldwide. Be at peace.

Tuesday: A New World Economic Order

There was no poverty among them, because people who owned land or houses sold them and brought the money to the apostles to give to others in need. (Acts 4:34-35, NLT)

Poverty, too, is violence. Recognize that the earth is not the source of lack. Lack is created in the human heart.

Pray to empower champions of a new day. Pray for architects of abundance who sustain rather than pillage the earth. Pray for a just distribution of the earth's resources. Pray for the eradication of poverty in our lifetime. Pray for agencies and organizations who serve the poor. Pray for the conviction of those who are wealthy to share with those in need. Pray for daily bread for the elderly, the sick and the wounded, and for children everywhere.

Wednesday: The Renewal of the Earth

"You are worthy, O Lord our God,
*   to receive glory and honor and power.*
For you created everything,
*   and it was for your pleasure that they exist*
*   and were created."*
—Revelation 4:11 (NLT)

When God gifted humanity with the earth, it was all good. Because of our negligent, self-serving stewardship, it has become exceedingly bad. Pray for the cleansing of the earth from toxins and pollutants. Pray for reforestation worldwide. Pray for the flourishing of endangered species. Pray for healthy drinking water for all. Pray for an end to the graffiti plundering of neighborhoods. Pray for the disarming of land mines. Pray for the church to take an active and visible leadership position in the renewal of the earth.

Thursday: The Church of Jesus Christ

When the heavy lead cover was lifted off the basket, there was a woman sitting inside it. The angel said,

"The woman's name is Wickedness," and he pushed
her back into the basket and closed the heavy lid again.
(Zechariah 5:8, NLT)

The gospel of Jesus Christ is mocked in the west, persecuted in the east, isolated in the north, and plagued in the south. Pray the apostolic prayers of Paul in the epistles. Pray for bishops, pastors, and leaders. Pray for missionary zeal. Pray for evangelistic fire. Pray for a manifestation of prophetic purpose in the earth. Pray to raise up a new generation for Jesus Christ. "Pray without ceasing." The body of Jesus Christ must stand in the earth as the light of God. "Do not cease to cry out to the LORD our God for us, and pray that he may save us" (1 Samuel 7:8, NRSV).

Friday: The Healing of the Sick

Bless the LORD, O my soul,
And forget not all His benefits:
Who forgives all your iniquities,
Who heals all your diseases,
Who redeems your life from destruction,
Who crowns you with lovingkindness and
*   tender mercies,*
Who satisfies your mouth with good things,
So that your youth is renewed like the eagle's.
—Psalm 103:2-5 (NKJV)

Prepare an altar with candles and a flask of healing oil on either side of the Word of God. Go to war! Fight the spirit of infirmity with the name, the blood, and the word of Jesus. "Put on the whole armor of God" (Ephesians 6:11, NRSV). Believe God for miracles.

Select one or more concerns each Friday:

- Make a list of the sick known to you and pray for them by name.
- Use the telephone directory to identify hospitals, clinics, hospices, places of therapeutic care, nursing homes, and convalescent centers. Pray for the patients who reside there.

- Use a medical reference book to identify and pray for the healing of those afflicted with all diseases. If you know specific names of persons with particular conditions, pray for them and their conditions by name.
- Pray for diligent and compassionate pharmaceutical companies.
- Pray for health care professionals.
- Pray for resources for those who want to attend medical school.
- Using your world map, identify and pray for the healing of regional diseases such as malaria in Africa and diabetes in India. Uproot the pandemic of HIV/AIDS in the world by your warfare intercession.
- Commit to memory as many healing Scriptures as you are able.

Saturday: Apostolic Benediction

May the God of peace himself sanctify you entirely; and may your spirit and soul and body be kept sound and blameless at the coming of our Lord Jesus Christ. (1 Thessalonians 5:23, NRSV)

By now you realize that intercession takes you out of your circumstances and positions you where God is at work in the world. Each of us is given a remarkable power to bless others. When offered in full faith consciousness and received in gratitude, blessing has great effect. It can change the mood of the receivers, renewing their minds and activating their hope. Bless others often. Include those whom you feel may dislike or resent you. Be intentional about asking God to bless the aged, strangers, pregnant women, and the disabled.

When we ask God to bless others, our own souls are refreshed. Somehow the world is made a better place. The hope within you can heal the hurt of so many. Remember that your capacity and opportunities to bless are limitless. You may write the blessings or call one to an unexpecting neighbor. You may sing your blessings or confer them with the laying on of hands.

"Blessed is everyone who blesses you" (Numbers 24:9, NRSV).

Sunday: Hope

This is the Lord's Day, a "little Easter," as my husband so often says. A day for wonder and amazement.

"Blessed are those who trust in the LORD and have made the LORD their hope and confidence." (Jeremiah 17:7, NLT)

Unlike every other day, when your attention was on the human condition and all of its challenges, this is the day to let go and worship the Lord. Let your expressions of love for God overflow from your heart to your lips. Try to imagine the great love that God has already expressed to you. Respond to any pain or discomfort with a praise offering in your heart! Allow the joy of the Lord to strengthen your hope. Remembering the resurrection, listen to praise music, dress to uplift your spirits, and make a few calls to people who live alone.

The Lord's love never ends.
  His mercies never stop.
They are new every morning.
  Lord, your loyalty is great.
I say to myself, "The Lord is what I have left.
  So I have hope."
The Lord is good to those who hope in him.
  He is good to those who seek his help.
  —Lamentations 3:22-25 (NCV)

I am mindful that sickness can take a toll on any marriage. I've seen some break down under the weight of it, while others were marvelously transformed. You may feel less than desirable, but never push your husband away or shut down honest communication. The stress on your husband will also escalate. An increase in domestic responsibilities as well as financial concerns will be added to his regular pastoral duties and schedule. Encourage him to see to his own self-care. Also, by scheduling regular quiet time together, you can allow the Holy Spirit to minister to your marriage.

Intercession will cause you to maintain a godly frame of mind. This alone will sanctify your disposition, give release, and fortify the hope that is in you. The overflow into your marriage will be the peace of God. Pray that your husband will love you without being intimidated by your present condition. Speak to each other in "psalms and spiritual sayings" that God's power can be made perfect. Pray continuously.

May your understanding of intimacy be transformed. May you know how to commune with deep passion and affection in profound gentleness, satisfaction, and sweetness. May your lights brighten and illumine each other. May you have no regrets. I hold you both in my heart, and my hope is for your eternal healing.

Now may the God of peace who brought back from the dead our Lord Jesus, . . . by the blood of the eternal covenant, make you complete in everything good so that you may do his will, working among us that which is pleasing in his sight, through Jesus Christ, to whom be the glory forever and ever. Amen. (Hebrews 13:20-21, NRSV)

Death

"Blessed are those who mourn, for they shall be comforted."
(Matthew 5:4, NKJV)

My dear Shalom,

The dead do not know the sting of death. But for those who remain, it is almost palpable. While there is great focus on resurrection in our churches, there is little, if any, discussion of death and dying. Our virtual silence has created an acute gap in our faith formation. It is far easier to confess supernatural intervention and miraculous faith or refuse to receive any negative doctor's reports than it is to prepare ourselves for death.

Yet, inevitably death comes—unwanted, inconvenient, and unreasonable. After death's work is done, we are left to try to understand its meaning, the source of its triumph, and how we will survive its arrival. Our thoughts are murky, our emotions blurred, our movements robotic. The breath has passed from us, and hope has become a lonesome stranger. We are left without anchor, compass, or sail.

So it is with you, my dear sister. Just yesterday, you were first lady. But today your title has been changed to widow. Today, without assignment, flock, or post, you have become yourself, a woman of tender needs and fragile means. Today, you mourn.

Today, you cry out to the empty pillow beside you, the empty chair opposite you, the empty robe hung in the bathroom. The vows of covenant clergy marriage allow only death the authority to separate us. Not sickness, poverty, disappointment, or betrayal; only death can dissolve our union.

Give yourself time to systematically transition from wife to widow to a woman of purpose, meaning, and value. In time, the part of your soul that died with him can experience resurrection. While you restore yourself into wholeness, consider taking a sabbatical from the church where your husband was pastor. You need space to grieve and to heal. You need rest from years of active ministry and the time you may have devoted to being a full-time caregiver to your ailing spouse. You need space to rediscover your interests, unexplored talents, and abilities. You need a place of refuge.

Take time to grieve. You may listen to one of his sermons and it will feel like he is not gone. That is, until the sermon ends and the emptiness sucks the marrow out of your bones. It will hit you once again that death has cheated you. When his birthday, your anniversary, and the holidays come around, you will miss his physical presence especially.

When you are ready, seek help in identifying those services and agencies that are available to you to enrich the quality of your life. Life will not be the same, and neither will you. You are a woman who has known what it means to be loved and cherished. You have had a hand to hold at midnight and a sunrise companion, an intercessor, a priest, and a friend. You must take time to acknowledge your loss. Suppression will only allow your grief to fester.

And I looked, and behold a pale horse: and his name that sat on him was Death. (Revelation 6:8, KJV)

Scripture reminds us that our witness is not to death, but rather, to life: "our Lord Jesus Christ . . . died for us, that whether we wake or sleep, we should live together with him" (1 Thessalonians 5:9-10, KJV).

The mystery of the gospel is that you and your husband both now live together with Jesus. By no means do I intend to spiritualize your very real human need to mourn; rather, I desire to call attention to the fact that while the redeemed of the Lord suffer the agonizing separation of death, we never suffer loss because we too are with Jesus. Reflect often on the above passage as you seek restoration through the mystery.

And if we have hope in Christ only for this life, we are the most miserable people in the world. (1 Corinthians 15:19, NLT)

There are three spiritual disciplines that will serve you well during this season of your life: spontaneity, simplicity, and sanctity. Some aspects of these disciplines may seem unorthodox; however, they will reawaken you to the depths of your inner life. They are designed to free you of the psychological mind-set engendered by your position as first lady. At the same time they will help you birth an identity that beautifully captures the new woman you are becoming. There will be a great temptation to exhale and simply live in your past. But I genuinely believe that God has something magnificent in mind concerning your future. Allow yourself to get excited about it.

Now, all glory to God, who is able to keep you from stumbling, and who will bring you into his glorious presence . . . with great joy. (Jude 24, NLT)

Crowned with Spontaneity

As a pastor's spouse, you have been shaped by a role, defined by tradition, and judged by external expectations. So much of your life has not been your own. As a result, you may have lost your ability to engage your spontaneous side. Your new status provides a perfect opportunity to adjust your life gauge. The impulse of the soul brings life. So do not bind your life with propriety or the superficial expectations imposed on you by others. Answer the call to joy. At first, you may feel as though you are acting on a whim or having an adolescent regression. Never mind trying to define your behavior. Allow yourself to go there. Life from now on can be an adventure. (Don't worry; you won't lose your salvation!)

Is your body unhappy with tailored suits? Does your hair want to be dyed red? Is the circle of mourners sapping your strength? Do you find yourself wondering what it would be like to take a yoga class in Bali? Are you in need of a fresh approach to worship? Want to try sushi, oxtails, or risotto? Need to take a train ride to nowhere? Sparks of enthusiasm should not be quenched. They are gems in your crown of spontaneity, coaxing you to break back into life. These sparks give you permission to wear blue mascara with a red suit, cover your body with lotion that glitters, or sign up for a gourmet cooking class.

You have had your night of weeping. It's morning! Rituals, roles, and protocol do not run your life anymore. You are a free agent. It's time to explore new meanings, to be compassionate with your shortcomings, and to excel at being your magnificent self. Break the rules! Whether you created them or ingested them from the atmosphere, their terms have expired.

A spontaneous life is lived facing the sun. It is unhurried and does not shun the impractical. It is a life where God is known and does not have to be proven. A spontaneous life brings forth a spontaneous spirituality, a life subject to both the passion and the glory of Jesus Christ. For you, the Holy Land is wherever you are led to commune with God. At a restaurant, a bus stop, a waiting room, under a tree, beside a pool. No place is off limits.

Spontaneous spirituality is an invitation to a cathedral where you and God abide alone and your adoration fills the entire space with light. It is the call to write a prayer for a high official in the church or government and leave it in a prayer box. It is taking a solitary prayer walk around a school to pray for the children, teachers, and their families. It is buying a dozen roses and giving them away one by one to those whom the spirit leads. It is sitting on a bench at the zoo praising God for all creation. It is standing naked in your shower and blessing every part of your body.

A life of spontaneous spirituality is a soul open to receive and embrace the impulse of the Holy Spirit immediately and without hesitation. It means giving full and indiscriminate expression of God's love, in whatever way the Holy Spirit guides.

Liberated by Simplicity

Until now, your life has been complicated by your clergy spousal duties, public affairs and church functions, church politics and church drama. Your new status can allow you to taste and see the goodness of the simple life. We are complex individuals living lives of information overload. We must find a way to climb out from under the deluge of messages, demands, and subliminal thoughts that assail us.

It would behoove you to sort out of your life those individuals, thoughts, and things that obscure the light. We are so busy and overextended that we fail to see how cluttered our lives have become. We romanticize our exhaustion and swamp our purpose with futile obligations. We are left with papers too insignificant to file and too seductive to throw away. The Holy Spirit cries out to us to simplify our lives. For only by simplicity can the earth be renewed. Simplicity pays homage to creation. It means letting go of those things that have lost meaning. Simplicity elegantly features the beauty of a precious few items in their fullness. Simplicity is the courage to create living space for your destiny. Simplicity is freedom. It is holy unto the Lord.

[S]he that hath two coats, let [her] impart to him that hath none; and [s]he that hath meat, let [her] do likewise. (Luke 3:11, KJV)

TIPS TO SIMPLIFY YOUR LIFE

Eliminate excess.

Downsize your living space.

Place a moratorium on shopping.

Eat natural, healthy foods.

Give away anything you have not worn in the past year.

Drive a car that you can afford.

Put credit cards away.

Pursue relationships that are meaningful.

Ask yourself the following question before making any purchase, attending any event, or entering into a relationship: Will it bring meaning to my life, beauty to my soul, health to my body, or prosperity to my finances? A simple yes or no answer will determine the nature of my decision.

Remember that you are creating space for your expansive soul. You are healing your energy. You now have breathing room, a gateway to enter your new world.

The heart and prayer of simplicity is gratitude. Gratitude is buoyant, holy, and liberating. Beginning and ending each day with a celebration of gratitude will diminish that gnawing sense of need and disarm any loitering spirit of consumerism. Gratitude brings amazement back into our lives and tames the beast of fear.

The Wings of Sanctity

The last prayer in the Bible, Revelation 22:20, pleads "Maranatha!" which means "Come, Lord Jesus." It is a prayer free of verbosity and vain display. This one word prays every concern of your heart, every need of your body, every issue of life. Whispering Maranatha is to stir the resolve of the angelic host. Even thoughts of Maranatha cause divine excellencies to flow in your direction. A Maranatha wrung from the anguished heart of a widow is enough to create a rainstorm of blessings. A joyous Maranatha will unleash power, cripple the antichrist, and throw open the gates of possibility.

Praying the Maranatha Prayer

Sit in the silence of morning. As you inhale, chant "Mara." As you exhale, chant "Natha." Be focused, unhurried, devoted, and free. No matter what distractions attempt to intrude, do not cease praying Maranatha. As you pray, your soul will be lifted high above any claim of suffering, disease, depression, or uncertainty. If you are faithful in praying this prayer, your soul will soar.

Pray Maranatha when you are lonely. Pray Maranatha when you are overwhelmed. Pray Maranatha if you are feeling insecure. And the Spirit of the Lord will surely come.

The presence of the Lord will be your highest joy. The presence of the Lord will be your soul assurance. The presence of the Lord will invoke radiance and majesty and wholeness in your life. You will soon decide for yourself that nothing can compare with being in the presence of God's extravagant glory.

And now he has made all of this plain to us by the appearing of Christ Jesus, our Savior, who broke the power of death and showed us the way to life and immortality through the Good News. (2 Timothy 1:10, NLT)

A Closing Word

Heaven is never further away than when it has claimed your beloved. Eternity is impossible to measure when counting the seconds that you are apart. To draw him nearer, you can plant a tree in the rainforest, provide for an orphan in India, donate books to a seminarian, light a candle on the date of his passing, or make a collage of pictures that tell his life story and present it to his grandchildren.

Thoughts of your husband are not a relapse. They are evidence of the heart's profound experience with a love that is everlasting. Imbibe the sweet taste of these memories as they pass by. Whisper benedictions to the wind. Grow strong, and turn the pages to the next chapter of your life. Our souls are not designed to be monuments to the dead. We bear a light that is greater than death itself. Let your faith formation be resplendent in the light of God. Endued with a new praying, trust yourself to make difficult decisions. For your inner healing and encouragement, this prayer was created:

Abba Shalom,
Impart to me dream realities of happiness.
Flood my soul with icons of blessing.
Draw my thoughts to heaven and set me free of fear—
Fear of sickness
Fear of poverty
Fear of loneliness
And fear of death.

Write your name in the hollow spaces of my heart, that
your love might emanate through me to the cosmos.
Consecrate my soul and
Drape me in the radiance of your eternal glory. Amen.

May the memory of your husband be as beautiful as a morning sky without rain. May the whispers of his scent, the shadow of his touch, and the echo of his voice bring a smile to your heart. He is gone, but don't stop dancing. Don't be ashamed to sing out loud the love songs of your journey together. A widow is a woman. And, because you are God's woman, beauty and laughter and love and song will radiate from your life.

LETTER 14

Repression

Then afterward
  I will pour out my spirit on all flesh;
your sons and your daughters shall prophesy
  your old men shall dream dreams
  and your young men shall see visions.
Even on the male and female slaves,
  in those days, I will pour out my spirit.
  —Joel 2:28-29 (NRSV)

Dear Huldah,

What's a prophet to do when she has been muzzled emotionally?
When the compelling urgency of the proclamation renders her
incoherent, frantic, suicidal, and horribly alone? Why would God
call her to preach and then abandon her to the atrocities of silence,
contempt, and anonymity?

Must humiliation be a prerequisite to holiness? Must being
cherished include condescension and public isolation? Are marriage and a prophetic vocation utterly irreconcilable when the wife
is also called?

Well, Huldah, I restate your question so that you will know that
I really do hear your heart, your hurt, and your hope. I can't imagine a state more potentially conflicted than that of wife and prophet.

Were it not for the effectual witness of Deborah, Isaiah's wife,
Dr. JoAnn Browning, Dr. Gloria White-Hammond, Dr. Elaine

113

McCollins Flake, the Rev. Marilyn Robinson, Dr. Jessica Ingram, and Dr. Claudette Copeland, I, too would believe the challenge to be insurmountable. These women learned by teaching themselves how to navigate seminary education, parenting, laundry, meals, and the needs of the local church pastored by their husbands.

> *"For truly I tell you, if you have faith the size of a mustard seed, you will say to this mountain, 'Move from here to there,' and it will move; and nothing will be impossible for you." (Matthew 17:20, NRSV)*

By faith, we are gifted with a life without boundaries, without limitations. The moment we say yes to the call of God, we are out of the box. Relapses are not uncommon given the religious culture and climate of our times. Nevertheless, we eventually come to realize that the call is not optional.

Fulfilling Two Responsibilities

To a large degree, you have two responsibilities. The first is to discern how much your perception of what it means to be a biblical wife handicaps your ability to be faithful to the call and the gift of God within you. In this same vein, what are the decisions that you make that limit your prophetic purpose?

Second, what is your husband's response to your calling—verbal and nonverbal? You believe that your marriage is ordained by God. This means that God has a vision for your gifts to flow together to the glory of the kingdom. Communication is the foundation of a healthy marriage and requires the participation of both persons.

I am certain that this is not a simple matter. The pastorate is drenched in all kinds of ego issues, which is probably why neither of you has dealt with the implications of your calling and gift. It is healthy that you have at least begun talking to yourself about the matter.

I spoke with my husband to find out from the male perspective the major hindrances to a pastor embracing the gift and call of his wife. Bishop John feels fairly confident that at least one or any combination of the following is involved: biblical interpretation of women in ministry, traditional understanding of the role of wife, and fear of competition in his own home.

Just one of these ruling the heart of a husband could mean all kinds of bondage for the wife. A combination of the three would spell disaster apart from the wisdom of God. I say with all due faith that you are absolutely in God's hands. As it is written, "The one who calls is the one who justifies." This is not a rationale for unscrupulous radicalism, theological posturing, or divorce! The matter has too many eternal ramifications. Therefore, what is needed are supernatural measures of the highest magnitude. Prevailing prayer will open a "door of utterance." Supernatural manifestations have the power to banish doubt. Apostolic intercession can break every yoke.

The gift and call of God upon your life are above all spiritual. I cannot overemphasize the importance and necessity of prayer for your spiritual health and to empower you to create a life of balance, beauty, and benediction. Trust God to honor your prayers with an undeniable anointing and irrevocable favor. God will so order your life and circumstances that even unbelievers will know that you are chosen, elect, and special. As the apostolic layering begins to unfold, you will enter such dimensions of spiritual power that the church worldwide will be benefited. In a little while, even soon, your beloved will see you as you really are. And in time, he too will rejoice. It would be futile to attempt to get ahead of God in this matter. Time belongs to God. So do not get caught up in vain and repetitious arguments.

> *The* LORD *will keep you from all evil;*
>   *he will keep your life.*
> *The* LORD *will keep*
>   *your going out and your coming in*
>   *from this time on and forevermore.*
>   *—Psalm 121:7-8* (NRSV)

"God does speak—sometimes one way and sometime another.

He speaks even though men may not understand it.
God may speak in a dream or a vision of the night.
This is when men are in a deep sleep and lying
in their beds."
—Job 33:14-15 (NCV)

You must plumb the depths of God with faith, consistency, and love. This is the most vital undertaking of your life on earth. Intend to persevere, "knowing that your labor in the Lord is not in vain." Your behavior will be intense but never irrational. You will be responsible in the world—in the care of your family, your person, and your employment. At the same time, you will remain accountable to God for spiritual maturity and integrity.

Marriage in this culture has been corrupted by materialism, erotic exploitation, fear of intimacy, and an inadequate prayer life. For the journey assigned to you, you must live God, a notion unfamiliar to present-day religionists. To live God is not given to those whose only claim to the supernatural is church membership. Nor is it given to the faint of heart, the spiritually or emotionally needy, or the parasitic. To live God, one must have faith and audacity.

If you and your marriage are to rise above the status quo of pride and repression, insecurity and vulnerability, shame and rage, resistance and accommodation, you must live God. Live God, not as the ancients did who fled to the wilderness, desert, or mountains. Rather, live God as a blazing thunder in the midst of the city with apostolic vision and integrity. To live God is to be liberated from the need for title, status, or approval. Live God unapologetically, fearlessly, and with a reconciling joy. You will dismantle hostility with your grace, permeate resistance with your compassion, withstand criticism with humility, and draw God closer with your praise. Live God, not in the resignation of Leah but in the consuming love of Mary Magdalene. Spirit speaks to spirit. Live God!

Who can fathom the soul of such a woman? Who can break her stride? Or cancel her visions? Embrace this prophetic code with the same devotion Jesus possessed when he humbled himself to be baptized by John.

- Let your prayer life be unrehearsed and authentic.
- Partake of Holy Communion with an openness to manifestation.
- Remove alcohol, nicotine, and narcotics from your life.
- Eliminate excess.
- Withhold your thoughts and tongue from gossip, jealousy, meanness, and condemnation.
- Unleash perpetual blessings upon others.
- Consecrate the gift of your sexuality unto your spouse.
- Embrace holiness as your chief joy.
- Give yourself to the love of God.
- Mature in wisdom, knowledge, and understanding of the Word of God.
- Give freely.
- Be aglow in the worship of the Lord.

By your apostolic intercession for him, your husband will receive a fresh revelation. You are his covenant bride; you are not the enemy, the competition, or a witness for the prosecution. The mind of God has conceived this thing! And the mind of God will reveal it. Defend it, upbuild it, and manifest it. The kingdom intent and content of your marriage is more than procrastination can delay, theology can define, liturgy can master, or history can predict. This marriage is a supernatural phenomenon. Let Wisdom tutor you. Let laughter comfort you. Let God breathe in you a world of sanctification. And as for you, love your husband.

Receiving Discernment

I have no clear understanding of how God is made known to you. Nor do I have a real sense of your comfort level when it comes to penetrating the realm of the mystery. What happens when you are alone with God? Are you awake or sleep? Is God's communication with you by way of a voice, a presence, an impression, a bodily sensation, a knowing? Or by some other means? It was different for Moses, Ezekiel, Zechariah, Mary, and Paul. Pay attention to the way God chooses to come to you. Make a note of it; even after the fact. Perhaps a thread will emerge.

As God's prophet, one must be at home in the supernatural realm in order to receive discernment, revelation, and credible utterance. Life in God must provide the impetus for your journey. Cause your soul to be housed by the Holy Ghost as through personal examination you identify and release everything that is an affront to your divinity. For you, humility must become a sacrament, lest you be misguided by ego and the flesh. In matters of the Spirit, it must be God who justifies, God who "opens a door of utterance," God who makes room for your gift and calling. The mantra for those who desire to humble themselves must be "Only God." Spend a day or just an hour with this as your focus and meditation: "Only God."

Without humility, one can never benefit from the reality of God's presence, rest secure in the love of God, or endure hard trials with radical hope. To be authentic, humility must come from the deepest place within your soul. Unlike passivity, it is noble. Nor are the truly humble doormats. They are a fountain of grace in a world that lacks patience, compassion, reverence, generosity, and kindness. Humility is strength surrendered to God. It is something we must ask God for, because we do not possess it naturally. "The reward of humility and the fear of the LORD are riches, honor and life" (Proverbs 22:4, NASB).

In receiving discernment about your call, as in your marriage, live God! Live God, and you will not be moved by setups, letdowns, saboteurs, misrepresentations, or any of the words or works of the ungodly.

. . . for the word of God, and for the testimony of Jesus Christ . . . (Revelation 1:9, KJV)

Prophesy the return of Christ.
Prophesy with dominion and authority to shape and shake the nations.
Prophesy with apostolic hope to raise up the body of Jesus Christ in the midst of rubble and destruction.

Prophesy with unfettered tongue to the oppressors, the
   predators, the abusers, the excluders, the diminishers,
   the demeanors, the derelicts, and the demon-possessed!
Let the word in you become a tsunami of healing in
   the earth.
Let God in you shatter all idolatry.
Be the pouring of the Lord that fills every crack and every
   crevice with the light of God!
And then

Be still, and know that I am God!
   I am exalted among the nations
      I am exalted in the earth. (Psalm 46:10, NRSV)

Caring for Your Mind

I must speak to you very plainly about what it means to live in the
light of the darkness of God. By your experience, you have learned
well that God's ways are not our ways and God's thoughts are not
our thoughts (see Isaiah 55:8). Yet this in no wise provides even a
glimpse of the absolute otherness of the almighty God. An ant has
a greater capacity to behold the ocean than we do to comprehend
the magnitude, the majesty, or the movement of our sovereign
Lord. With our eyes, we cannot fully behold God. And with our
ears, the voice of the Lord is barely audible. We are, as it were, inebriated by a mystery, and so the passion of our souls is exumed
from all deaths:

   the death of purpose
   the death of personality
   the death of presence
   the death of procrastination
   the death of prophetic vision.

Life within us is stirred. It is both tangible and invisible. Because
we are of the dust, it is dusty. Because we are imperfect, it is
incomplete. And because with our hearts we have loved without

conscience, deceived without repentance, and resisted the teachings of Jesus, we lack courage to allow God to stand up in us. Nevertheless, this beauteous darkness is not kept from us.

Some are not certain what I mean by the darkness of the God whom we know as the light of the world. Well, God's silence is God's darkness. Also, God's hiddenness is God's darkness. God's immutability is dark. Also God's lyrics and God's movement and God's laughter! All darkness to we who cannot comprehend or articulate or overtake any of the above.

In this season, perhaps you may experience your marriage as in the realm of the darkness of God. To which I say, "Fear no evil." Drink early of your sacrament of humility. Trusting God's love and God's purpose for you and your marriage will be your strength. My dear Huldah, I know the spirit of desperation has the power to blind us to the hand of God moving on our behalf. Or what is worse, it can unleash a flood of depression. Spirit is so powerful. You must intend to take care of your mind. Anchor your thinking in the reality of God's love for you. Sit with this inward affirmation as a daily reminder and encouragement: "I am an incarnation of God's divine idea." As you allow this truth to gently penetrate your mind, your heart, and your soul, the effect should be serenity and assurance.

This affirmation gives you the power and the authority to deflect all condemnation. Furthermore, it empowers you to short-circuit any negative thoughts or moods. Never sit with depression. Get up and move. Praise dancing, a prayer walk, housecleaning, car washing, anything in the way of physical movement awakens positive energy. If you find depression unmanageable and unresponsive to your efforts, talk to your physician or a mental health professional. You may require medication. It is nothing to be ashamed of. My testimony is that medication has dramatically improved my quality of life. And I am so thankful to God. St. Teresa and St. Augustine are known to have suffered with bouts of depression. Pray to the Lord to grant you the wisdom and clarity to make healthy decisions. Quite often our minds are not up to the things of the Spirit.

For this reason, it is important to have a spiritual director as you pursue your faith formation. This person is much more than a prayer partner. He or she is someone who lives with the things of God daily. Someone you trust to speak into your spirit, whether a word of wisdom, encouragement, or chastisement. Someone who has no emotional investment in the outcome of the decisions you make. You chart the map under the guidance of the Holy Spirit. The spiritual director only helps you identify the landmarks.

At this point, I know only of the Roman Catholic Church and the Episcopalians to have a vocation in spiritual direction. Again, do not be a hostage to denominationalism. Spiritual direction could provide the objective, confidential environment you desire. However, if you experience it as intrusive, disconnected, uncomfortable, or frustrating, you can terminate the process. Spiritual direction is rarely cost-prohibitive. Look at it as an opportunity for a new experience. Be open to a journey that could prove to be life-changing.

> *Don't copy the behavior and customs of this world, but let God transform you into a new person by changing the way you think. Then you will know what God wants you to do, and you will know how good and pleasing and perfect his will really is.* (Romans 12:2, NLT)

Genius is a heavenly gift. Yet so often we know not how to incorporate it into our spiritual journey. Our thoughts and imaginations are often highly susceptible to the apocalyptic. We can be moved beyond our grounding if we are not attentive to our need for rest, stress reduction, and a quiet space. Avoid the companionship of demon chasers, prophets who are not subject to those who have authority over them, or bitter women who are afraid to love or be loved. You need your mind—whole, fresh, resilient, and expansive—to the glory of God.

If I have failed to acknowledge that the hurt is real, that enduring friendships are few, that loss can be unbearable, it was not to deceive you but to keep you from discouragement. An angry bed is a greater torment than an empty one. I know this. What I also know is that God heals. At first imperceptibly, then gently, then completely. You and your husband are a significant part of something too grand for pettiness, too glorious for vanity, and too life-changing for either of you to walk away from. God in him already knows that you are gifted, called, and remarkable. God in him is at war with every system, ideology, and fear that is at work to prevent the melding of your destiny! Know this, and allow your thoughts to take hold of it. Do not concern yourself with those who perceive your obedience to God as an assault on the ministry of your husband. They do not know the kingdom. Your mind will be safe as long as you continue to live God. Only then can you be free of the influence of warring personalities and hindering spirits. You will come to a place in God of such everlasting freedom that you receive the power to forgive, to pursue new beginnings, and to love unconditionally. Believe that you are well able to make this journey.

> *You chart the path ahead of me*
>   *and tell me where to stop and rest.*
>   *Every moment you know where I am. . . .*
> *You both precede and follow me.*
>   *You place your hand of blessing on my head. . . .*
> *I can never escape from your spirit!*
>   *I can never get away from your presence! . . .*
> *If I ride the wings of the morning,*
>   *if I dwell by the farthest oceans,*
> *even there your hand will guide me,*
>   *and your strength will support me.*
>   —*Psalm 139:3, 5, 7, 9-10* (NLT)

Our thoughts can bring us heaven on earth. Or with our minds we can trap ourselves into the deepest purgatory. Renew your mind with beauty. Stimulate an awareness of the textures, colors, forms, and life sources in the world around you. Indulge your sensibilities in poetry and art. Luxuriate in new music, new rhythms, new sounds, lyrics drawn by purpose, justice, hope, glory, and joy. Immerse yourself in the balm of nature. And above all, don't ever forget to love yourself, to love God, to love your husband. To love others is a sham for the one who has not learned to love herself. The glow emanating from your heart is simply divine. You are Huldah, eclectic, extravagant, exotic. Embrace the wonder of you! God has to be proud when God considers Huldah. You are one of a kind!

And you, O tower of the flock,
hill of daughter Zion,
to you it shall come,
the former dominion shall come,
the sovereignty of daughter Jerusalem.
—Micah 4:8 (NRSV)

Body Image/Sexuality

I am fearfully and wonderfully made . . .
And that my soul knows very well.
—Psalm 139:14 (NKJV)

Dear Leah,

Every part of you, mind, body, and spirit, your past, your present, and your future, are all within the sphere of God's wonderful grace. Gather yourself together from the four winds of fear, change, uncertainty, and insecurity. You are an emissary of soul— a woman alive, a beauty unstained. You have been kissed by eternity. There is none like you, nor shall there ever be! Nor shall there ever be! "Rejoice in the Lord always. Again I will say, rejoice!" (Philippians 4:4, NKJV).

Consider the life and power of the soul. Who can measure its dimensions? Who can weigh its strengths? What sorrow can outlast the frontiers of its infinite pardon? Soul is the seat of conscience, will, discernment, and divine propensities. Soul aligns us with God, shatters all delusions, and causes us to aspire to genius, immortality, and perfect love. We are emissaries of the soul. It is the region of our highest self. The self beyond which there is only God, heaven, and eternity. You are a woman beloved, and yet you find no beauty in yourself to cling to, to honor, to embrace, or to celebrate. You cannot even see yourself through the eyes of the one who loves you most.

Your poor body image is interfering with your sexual freedom and enjoyment. Lovemaking should not be work for either of you. But shame and embarrassment have a way of crowding the marriage bed.

We owe a debt of gratitude and compassion to our earthly bodies. In every state of life their beauty must be free to shine, to glow. Even if never before, then surely now is the time to begin to enjoy your body, to celebrate and discover your sexual personality.

I say this in the presence of almighty God "in whom we live and move and have our being." We are created for passion. Unfortunately, the rhythm of our lives is out of sync with any vision of health or serenity. The intensity of our schedules, the plethora of organizational demands, personal issues, and the resulting dysfunction that all of the above create in family life is bewitching. We are so out of touch with our bodies that we are actually puzzled when symptoms of disease emerge or when we lack the capacity to live sensually.

Who are you, dark mystery?
Tabernacle of secret fire imprisoned by icy theologies
    and fears
Created with an issue of blood
Hypnotized by a song
Entangled in a rhapsody of past-present sadness
Desperate for release
Flooded with dreams of ecstasy
Enchanted with night shadows expelling
    unfamiliar moans
Who are you, dark mystery?
Shrouded with memories of betrayal
Gasping to be cherished
Dancing to the silent lyrics of unknown songs of love
Reaching for God from the bottom of the sea
Glimpsing heaven in a kiss
Praying
Praying
Praying

Without sound or sanctuary
Until the two become one
Amen.

During this monumental turning point in your journey, choose to begin living in your body rather than simply through your body. You are oneness even as the blessed holy Trinity. This trinity is inseparable, divine continuity—body, soul, and spirit. Within you is the power to heal and reconcile your self. Within you is an untapped well of desire awaiting release. Gather your self together and be the woman: unashamed, free, and passionate. Covenant clergy marriage was never intended to be platonic!

Yet so many of us, in the name of holiness, were raised in a manner that disconnects us from our selves. And when our response to our own bodies is unfriendly, it makes for a very traumatic experience. In marriage, we are confronted with our body history, complexities, and culture daily. As a first lady, much to your regret, your body is a matter of public domain. Every pound lost or gained is documented in someone else's memory. All of that notwithstanding, you owe it to yourself to embrace the mystery and magic of your body and self.

Your spirituality does not flow separate and distinct from your physical personhood, although you so often live as though they are. The teaching that sexual intercourse is solely for reproductive purposes is archaic. I don't think even you really believe that. Your resistance to intimacy has much more to do with the fact that you are a woman who is alienated from her own body.

For the most part, you have embraced your faculties without restraint. Intelligence, knowledge, and critical thinking do not offend your faith. But know this: woman is not only mind or reason and spirit; woman is also created a sexual being. In covenant love, *eros* is holy, passionate imagination liberating, and every climax brings exaltation of the deepest magnitude. With the touch of your beloved, any part of you can be a gateway to orgasm—your neck, your ear, your arm, your thigh, your feet . . .

Every part of you is honorable; "therefore glorify God in your body" (1 Corinthians 6:20, NRSV). The human body is a wonder!

Yes, your body (temple) is a key element in the reintegration of the self. Small wonder that, in this culture, one of the most emotionally debilitating experiences for women is poor body image. It seems to be an albatross that never goes away. This spirit of shame is unwelcome at all times. It is even more so when we live out our lives in full public view. You have the power, if you will only unleash the love, to bless and rejuvenate your body (temple).

There are bodies in the heavens, and there are bodies on earth. The glory of the heavenly bodies is different from the beauty of the earthly bodies. (1 Corinthians 15:40, NLT)

Quite often, family secrets are the source of this unwieldy shame. Incest, molestation, or rape, when unacknowledged and unhealed, have a debilitating impact on our lives well into our adulthood. If this is so, you are not the only one. Find a way to talk about this with your husband. But above all, get the help you need to slay this dragon.

Leah, it's time for you to own your beauty. This is not vanity; it is gratitude. The transformation must take place in your own heart, in your own eyes. Look around at God's handiwork. How glorious it is! You are not the exception. It's time you unlearned the lessons of self-hatred and tutor yourself in self-discovery. A covenant wife is more than a hat, a lace handkerchief, and an assigned pew. A covenant wife cannot be reduced to a head table, an asterisk in programming, or a fixture of ecclesiastical protocol.

Surely, we are weavers of the mystery, whether with fine threads of silver or straw. We inhabit realms of bliss and realms of agony. From these we fashion the indelible memories of eternity. Indeed, we are one with the wonder of all creation. With our tears, we mirror the lyrics of the rain. In our hearts, we echo the song of the dove. We are as the sap from the trees, the ripples of a stream. We are as the dormant caterpillar. We are as the power of the lion. We are as the grandeur of the mountains. We are as the healing of ginger. We are as extraordinary as Saturn. And we are as unrepeatable as time itself. Eternity has come upon us. "[God has] set eternity in the human heart."

*Yet they cannot fathom what God has done from
beginning to end. (Ecclesiastes 3:11, NIV)*

Yes, you are unfathomable, even to yourself. How long will you
postpone loving the skin that you're in? When will your body be
worthy of your gratitude? In the whole of creation, everything has
its own beauty, purpose, and destiny. Consider the miracle of you,
Leah. Silence the noise of a past that you cannot change and create your own hymn of doxology.

We should not do for others from a sense of our own unworthi-
ness. Rather let us serve God out of the overflow of our own joy
and abundance. Duty without passion is void. Authentic love of
neighbor is an extension of self-love. You are a living soul, a
woman of excellence, yesterday's tomorrow. Know that you are
not powerless. You are a living soul. When we face the light of God,
we receive clarity, momentum, and grace for living. Each today
from now on will be as no other. Yet, for you, change need not be
ominous. You have available to you a range of self-care initiatives
that support your new self-understanding and encourage self-suf-
ficiency. Explore fresh options that promote the melding of mind,
body, and soul. It is admittedly an eclectic array of personal thera-
pies intended to invoke confidence. Never lose sight of the fact that
the Bible says, "Don't throw away your confidence" (see Hebrews
10:35). You have the power to create the life that will make you
happy! Do not give your power away! Take full advantage of your
knowledge of the fruit of the Spirit (see Galatians 5:22).

We have been gifted by heaven with these marvelous bodies, the
one place our souls are free to hang out. So it is with our bodies that
we begin. Return to the awareness of your body as the temple of
the Holy Spirit and all that *that* means. Begin to bless and consecrate your temple with deep and abiding thanksgiving. Thank God
for sight and touch and movement and breath and the beating of
your heart. Allow your fingers and toes to dance as you thank God.
Stretch in every direction that you are able to and thank God. Consider what every temple needs: an altar, light, music, and incense.
Envision your heart as God's altar, your eyes as reflecting the light
of God, your body as music, and your prayers as incense.

Maintain this awareness in your attitude, in your speech, and in your sense of presence. You are alive in the temple. Nourish, celebrate, strengthen, and honor your temple with all due consecration. This is holiness. Every time, within your heart, you genuflect before the throne of God, there comes a sacred communion with heaven. A golden inflowing of divine love. A transfiguration! Light from light. Radiance from glory. You are aglow with majesty! Hallelujah, this is a time to escalate oversight of your temple. To embrace your divinity. As Brother Lawrence teaches, "to practice the presence of God."

Now is the time to do something radical. Make a love offering to Jesus for the years of anguish that you spent oppressed by a tormenting spirit of inferiority when you accused yourself of being:

- too black
- too ugly
- too poor

Anoint your nakedness with eucalyptus oils of freedom until you are resplendent with grace and power—until you discover that you, too, have been given beauty for ashes.

> For we are the temple of the living God;
> as God said,
> "I will live in them and walk among them . . ."
> (2 Corinthians 6:16, NRSV)

It brings joy to the kingdom for the fullness of the Godhead to abide in a consenting consecrated vessel. How amazing is that— to finally experience the divinity within you, to have a union with God undefiled by doubt or resignation.

To realize the heaven in you.

To break free of the fraudulent criteria for beauty.

To join the hum of the ancients when your temple is ablaze with the light.

To recognize that in *this* body and not another you can know God!

There are so many ways available to us to honor, celebrate, and manifest the life of God in our bodies. They do not require a theological degree or prolonged asceticism. All that is needed is a healthy dose of self love.

Whether through videos, classes, or a personal trainer, begin practicing tai chi. It teaches one to reconnect with the breath. The movements are gentle and flowing. The pace is absolutely meditative. It is a wonderful self-gift to begin and end a day. It can be accompanied by nature sounds, hymns, or even classical music. Unbroken silence is golden when practicing tai chi. You will begin to know your body again in beautiful ways. Your posture, walking, and sitting will become more graceful. Gradually, you will gain a sense of inner tranquility and freedom. Most importantly, the spirit of heaviness will be lifted from your heart.

Our bodies are incredible. Within them is stored the memories of a lifetime of laughing, loving, hurting, fatigue, fear, fullness, hunger, thirst, pregnancy, birth, breastfeeding, dancing, waiting, and being awakened. Listen well to your body. Her vocabulary will increase as you discover new expressions of movement. As you unleash your creative passions, a whole new rhythm of life will be revealed to you. In that mode, detaching will become a simple process. Things will no longer hold power over you. You will no longer need to be surrounded by objects in order to feel secure. The treasure within you will begin to shine more and more and more. When we allow things to hold our lives hostage, we give the past permission to dominate and overrule the beauty available in the present moment. We nullify the prophetic purpose of our very existence. We are stuck! The best way to free ourselves is to let go of things and let God breathe refreshing into our lives.

Again, I must say, you will not regret bringing tai chi into your life. I can think of no better way to relearn how to live in your body. Tai chi provides for us a return to innocence, a return to awareness, a return to reverence and awe. We are as we are because slowly, systematically, we have come to embody the noise of inauthentic living. Forgetting that the essence of woman is a matter of the intangible rather than the material, we have yielded to the seduction of consumerism. Losing our integrity as specimens of divinity, compromising our status as "a little lower than the angels," we turned away from the Light.

But, once again, we can become the keepers of the secrets of God. Let us return to holy ground. This we begin with the restoration of the temple, the abode of God, the altar of sanctification. You have only to remember to bless your body daily and to live in your body.

The Benefits of Tai Chi

Tai chi empowers us to slow our lives down. Not in withdrawal, but through spiritual engagement. Tai chi, although a cultural venue of the East, has universal properties for the cleansing and renewal of the body. Tai chi easily adapts to Christian prayer and principles. It is not competitive or aerobic. Tai chi helps to maintain our connection with the rhythm of life. We re-embrace the mystery of our humanity. Tai chi invokes splendor, welcomes us into the realm of the soul. Tai chi unlocks compassion as it releases the movement of the breath.

Tai chi teaches us to center our awareness, to walk with integrity upon the earth. Tai chi renders us susceptible to the healing and grace of the Lord. Calling our inner selves into communion and harmony, we learn peace, oneness, and freedom. Indeed, we are "fearfully and wonderfully made . . . and that my soul knows very well" (Psalm 139:14, NKJV).

In the days ahead, I invite you to do something out of the box! You will need to buy seven long scarves that you can drape around your shoulders. Each one is to be a unique color, as indicated below. They are not intended to match what you are wearing. They have a much higher purpose. You will discover a set of Scriptures with each color. They are intended to ground and empower you. We all know about Noah's rainbow, a symbol of the promise of new beginnings. In that same spirit, I offer you Leah's rainbow.

For the days when your emotions need to be stimulated or repaired, wear *fuschia*. The energy from this color gives you a reason to smile. It brightens any skin tone. Wearing fuchsia can help ward off depression. Something about it connects with the human spirit and draws acknowledgment and affirmation from others. Post these Scriptures around your house and meditate on them: Psalm 92:12-15; Zephaniah 3:17; John 7:37-38; Romans 8:26-28; 15:4; .

When your energy is low—whether physical or emotional—try *chartreuse*. When you can't seem to get yourself going. When you feel internally bland, bare, lifeless, burned out, it may jump-start your spirit. Look at yourself in the mirror—you will smile. Breathe deeply and exhale any negative thoughts or feelings. Meditate on Psalm 141:1-2; Matthew 11:28-30; Mark 6:30-31; John 5:14; Philippians 3:12-14.

Amethyst is the color to wear when your desire and intention is to commune with the Lord. You use amethyst to remind yourself of God's holiness, to turn your thoughts toward the highest realm, to heighten your spiritual discernment. In this season, the altar of your heart is in continuous worship. If your physician permits, this is a wonderful day to fast, to pursue the light of God. Let your awareness affirm the miracles all around you. This is the day to forgive, to release everything that draws your attention away from God's love. This is the day of reconciliation in your heart—to your past, to those who have hurt or disappointed you, and most of all to your life purpose. Meditate on Psalm 93; 95; 108; Isaiah 45:21-22; Matthew 6:25-33; 2 Corinthians 5:17; 6:16; 7:1; Hebrews 11:6; James 3:14-18.

Aquamarine—just saying the name of this color is like an invocation. When your prayer is for the healing of the Lord. Inner healing. The healing of your body. The healing of your expectations. When what you desire of God is restoration. To be made whole. Mercy and "grace" are the gifts that await you as you seek the favor of the Lord! Meditate on Psalm 112; Isaiah 53:4; Matthew 9:27-31; Acts 11:16-18.

Orange is the color of magnetism, creativity, and imagination. Wear orange to enliven your confidence—to give you courage, boldness. When you need to learn to be a risk taker. To break out of the familiar. To embrace unexpressed areas of your personality. To honor your own magnificence. Meditate on Proverbs 18:5-9, 24; Acts 2:4; Colossians 4:5; Hebrews 10:35.

Wear *gold* when you desire to draw and share abundance, to eliminate debt, to generate fresh streams of income. The gold scarf should be worn when you have a fresh desire to sow into the kingdom and expand your missionary outreach. This is the time to pray in faith for divine order in your finances and the ability to increase your tithes. Meditate on Psalm 23:1; Proverbs 28:19-27; Isaiah 55; Matthew 6:25-34; John 10:10; 2 Corinthians 1:8-11; 9:6-11.

Wear *indigo* when you need wisdom. When you are faced with difficult decisions. When you need a ruling from God. When struggling with legal matters. When you need sound advice or good counsel, indigo is for you. Indigo has a certain majesty and strength. It is an excellent color to wear when you need a sense of protection. Meditate on Psalm 19:7; Proverbs 4:6-9; 13:10; Hosea 14:9; 1 Corinthians 1:25; James 1:5.

When you awaken in the morning, your spirit will tell you which scarf to wear. Pray this prayer or some other affirmation as you place the scarf around your shoulders, whether you remain at home or go out: "Lord Jesus Christ, Son of the living God, I place this scarf around my neck today to remind myself that you are my source of:

1. Encouragement . . . fuschia
2. Energy . . . chartreuse
3. Holiness . . . amethyst
4. Healing . . . aquamarine
5. Confidence . . . orange
6. Abundance . . . gold
7. Wisdom . . . indigo

"I recognize that the scarf itself has no power;
nor does the color necessarily have any biblical significance.
I employ these symbols to help me maintain

an active awareness of God's presence
and God's love for me.
My prayer and expectation today is
that the Word, purpose, and
light of God will be manifested
in my life in the name of Jesus.
Amen."

Let your intention be to actively honor the Lord in all that you say and think and do. Be open to "ordinary" miracles. Refuse to allow any preconceived notions to dwarf your enthusiasm. Buy back your joy through acts of kindness toward others. Be creative with your scarfing. Let your imagination run wild. Remember, it's God's secret. And you don't have to let on to anybody else. Throughout your day, allow the sight of the scarf and the texture of the scarf to call to mind God's presence, God's Spirit, and the Word of God. To live scentually, spray a small amount of essence on the ends of your scarf: lavender, sandalwood, jasmine, vanilla, amber, rose, patchouli, ylang-ylang, or one of the many varieties of citrus. Note what feelings they evoke, and then use them accordingly.

Again, do not let your outfit, but rather your spirit, determine which scarf you wear. Because, after all, it is your personal call to supplication, which means that you can wear the same color as often as you need to. "May our Lord Jesus Christ himself and God our Father, who loved us and by his grace gave us eternal encouragement and good hope, encourage your hearts and strengthen you in every good deed and word" (2 Thessalonians 2:16-17, NIV).

Dear Leah, may there be a seamless existence between your body, mind, and spirit. May you risk into your passion. May you take pleasure in your own nakedness. May you delight in the body of your husband. May you explore each other's mysteries. May the oils of your desire lubricate your souls. May your marriage bed be a healing space. May holiness roar from your ecstasy. May your blinded eyes be opened for you to see your divinity. May the colors of your supplication lead you to rapture. May your marriage be an implosion of fidelity.

How graceful are your feet in sandals,
   O queenly maiden!
Your rounded thighs are like jewels,
   The work of a master hand. . . .
How fair and pleasant you are,
   O loved one, delectable maiden!
You are stately as a palm tree,
   and your breasts are like its clusters.
I say I will climb the palm tree . . .
—*Song of Solomon 7:1, 6-8 (NRSV)*

From Desolation to Enchantment

Prayers for the Journey

Come, ye disconsolate, where're ye languish.
Come to the mercy seat, fervently kneel.
Here bring your wounded hearts, here tell your anguish;
earth has no sorrow that heav'n cannot heal.
—Thomas Moore (1816)

Prayer is perhaps the most discussed and least understood experience in faith formation. That may be because it is so unpredictable. Praying can be juicy, raw, illuminating, dull, effortless, difficult, and amazing all in the same day. When we step back from the temptation to be analytical, profound, or spiritual, we can be successful in our praying. If we are too self-aware, the prayer becomes an outlet for vanity rather than an authentic desire to hear from God. All matters of the heart are appropriate topics for prayer. Contrary to some theological approaches, we can relax in the presence of the Lord. Posture, attire, and vocabulary are insignificant. Try to understand and experience prayer as a way of loving and being loved. Even when you believe that you are out of time, you can pray as though you have all the time in the world! Not even time can separate you from the love of God. Take comfort in knowing that your prayers never die.

There is not a soul so positioned for healing as a soul prostrate in prayer. There is not a life so entrapped in turbulence that it cannot be gentled by a simple invocation. Our season on earth is a brief one. Nevertheless, the depth and breadth and height of our worldview depend on divine communion. Prayer happens when our hearts awaken to the presence of the Lord. Prayer happens when our knowing is infused with the mind of Christ, when God's passion becomes our passion, when we are transfigured by the light.

Each spiritual discipline is formulated for one fundamental purpose—prayer. The Scriptures teach that we have the capacity to "pray in the Spirit at all times in every prayer and supplication" (Ephesians 6:18, NRSV). The prayers that follow provide an opportunity for both. Do not be bound to the text; let the Holy Spirit lead you. Let grace assist your improvisation. When you don't know what to pray, perhaps these prayers will be helpful. Be guided by your own soul needs and desires.

When he had taken the scroll, the four living creatures and the twenty-four elders fell before the Lamb, each holding a harp and golden bowls full of incense, which are the prayers of the saints. (Revelation 5:8, NRSV)

Breathed by Silence

Be silent before the Lord GOD!
For the day of the LORD is at hand;
the LORD has prepared a sacrifice,
he has consecrated his guests.
—Zephaniah 1:7 (NRSV)

1.

Dear Holy Spirit,
Please teach me silence.
The noise within me is so great.
The noise without so dense.

Let your silence draw rest to my body,
that the fatigue will cease.
Show me the angels of Yahweh
so that I will not be afraid anymore.
Amen.

2.

My Lord,
You are God, and yet the song of your mystery
is a dirge in my heart.
My mind cannot grasp you.
My longing does not reach you.
Yet, I am desolate in my love for you.
Desperate to have you near.
Fumbling when I speak of you.
Lost, when I think I have found you.

And so I wait in the silence with my whole heart
and strength and will to hear your voice
to feel your breath as a passing shadow.
To plunge into the ecstasies of your silence.
But who can know you? Delineate the way of your providence?
Follow the echo of your footsteps?

Are there no windows through which
I may glimpse your secrets?
No mirrors in which your reflection can comfort me?
Is there no cleft, no cavern, no catacomb in which the relics
of your mercies may be found?

And yet you live . . .
Eternally,
Infinitely,
Sovereignly within. (Selah)

3.

Today, I acknowledge God's loving kindness.
Today, I soar beyond the limitations created by my dysfunction.
Today I am.
I am who I have become.
I am becoming. I am the guest of silence.

4.

Most holy and sweet Mystery,
You call me to be attentive to your presence,
as Mary who sat at your feet.
I must "be still, and know that [you] are God"
(Psalm 46:10, NRSV).

The gifting of your royal presence demands that I prostrate
myself and pour upon you the precious ointment of praise
and worship.

You are here, and I have nothing to give you
save a cauldron of excuses, rationalizations, and blaming.

Since you never accepted them before, this time I will
give you the silence that you have asked for. (Selah)

5.

Lord, Jesus Christ, Son of the living God,
I embrace the silence, and we are one.
We are holy.
We are breath.
The breath is fire, and I am ablaze
with the healing of divine love.
Thank you. Amen.

6.

Majesty of the cosmos,
Eternal love ablaze with redemption,
Because you are the bright and morning star; I pray the
radiance of your light transform and heal my inner life.
Even now, Lord Jesus, even now.

That ever I would be aglow and nations through me
the Lord would know.
God help me to walk uprightly.

Your great power comes alive in me in the beautiful silence.
The beautiful silence comforts this servant of the Lord.
The beautiful silence heals my life for joy.
So when I come to God in prayer, my thirst is quenched, my
heart repaired because you are the beautiful silence. Amen.

7.

"I am the gate." (John 10:9, NRSV)

*"For a wide door for effective work has opened to me, and
there are many adversaries." (1 Corinthians 16:9, NRSV)*

*After this I looked, and there in heaven a door stood open!
And the first voice, which I had heard speaking to me like
a trumpet, said, "Come up here, and I will show you
what must take place after this." (Revelation 4:1, NRSV)*

That which calls to me beyond the silence fills me
with awe and amazement.

The world beyond the silence is unknown to me.
How will I sustain myself; survive the unknowable?

I am wretched with anticipation without sign or wonder,
faith exhorts me to believe, to endure, and to wait.

Only the silence has begun to break, arresting my patience,
taunting my volition, provoking my fragile humility.

I remember, Jesus wept (John 11:35). So I join him.

"When the Lamb opened the seventh seal, there was silence
in heaven for about half an hour." (Revelation 8:1, NRSV)

In the Beginning Silence
The movement of the universe. This is the Light.
The passion of the heavenlies. This is the Light.
The rhythm of the moons. This is the Light.
The song of infinity. This is the Light.
All descend upon the soul of mortality as the sound of silence.
Oneness.
The end of all divisions. Healing!
The washing of all separations. Healing!
The purging of resistance. Healing!
A reggae synthesis unfolds. The Light is the healing.
Union.
Communion.
Celestial radiance.

The glow of silence
Crescendos of overflowing magnificence.
Amen.

The cosmic fulfillment of dreams and visions.
Amen.

The once-dead, now-alive greet the living with halos
gathered as a bouquet.
Amen.

The scream of new life, eternal life, penetrates heaven
like a golden silence.
Amen.

A lightning bolt of happy.
A hurricane of praise.
And every ever-living being exhales in silence.
Amen. Amen. Amen.

Restless Soul, Dreamless Thoughts

"ask for the ancient paths,
where the good way lies; and walk in it,
and find rest for your souls."
—Jeremiah 6:16 (NRSV)

1.

Lord, I will call upon your name as long as I have breath.
I will attune my thoughts to your presence.
With my heart and my strength, I chase after the living God.
I welcome you, spirit of Yahweh.
I give honor, deep regard and hallowed reverence
to the name of Jesus.
Today is my day of new beginnings. I shall speak the names
of the Lord with the tongues of my heart.
I can never be weaned from Abba's breast.
Your glory is the milk of eternal life.
My desire is holy, complete, and flawless.
I am restless for your presence.
Until you come, my soul is a desolate wasteland,
my spirit a rigid carcass.
Breathe your life into me. Abide with me.
I know you will come.
My soul has captured the scent of your approach.
I cry out to you to hurry!

Divinity is too slow for my eager heart.
Come close, dear God, and taste of my desire.
Cover me with the blanket of your mysteries
and shatter my fears forever.
Amen.

2.

Kairos is true.
The anointing is true. The fire is true.
Lord, speak to me powerfully concerning the path.
Your voice is not clear to me.
Your will is clouded by my emotions.
I feel trapped in an elevator stuck between floors.
It seems I can neither rise nor descend.
My every attempt to change is frustrated by uncertainty.
I am not sure who I am or who you want me to be.
The past has overtaken my world like a cruel despot;
it reigns without compassion.
I don't have the energy to rebel against it.
Lord Jesus Christ, Son of the living God, have mercy upon me.
Amen.

3.

Out of the depths I cry to you, O LORD.
Lord, hear my voice!
Let your ears be attentive
to the voice of my supplications!
—Psalm 130:1-2 (NRSV)

My agonies are seen and known by you.
The ejaculations for life, deliverance, joy, healing, and love
have all been made in your name, Jesus.
Have I not been as a watchman on red alert
or a nurse in the intensive care unit?
Vigilant for any sign, I neither sleep nor slumber.

Have you forgotten me?
Have I just plain missed you?
Or can it be that you are not yet ready to answer?

Without wanting to; I will wait. This is not the path
that I would have chosen for myself; but I will wait.
If the answer itself is in the waiting, so be it.
Amen.

4.

Lord, are you walking around my prayers? Circling them?
Viewing them from every perspective?
I don't want to live in torment anymore.
I have poured myself out. I have nothing else to give.
I am weary, drained, empty.
You knew this time would come. Help me. Please help me.
Or there will be no help for me.
God, you know everything please do something.
My life is shattering.
Say something, anything so that I may have life after all of this.
Amen.

5.

When the word of the Lord to you is "trust";
all you have is the word of the Lord.
For easier it is to forgive than to ever trust again.

"Trust in the Lord, *and do good." (Psalm 37:3,* NRSV)

*"Trust in the Lord with all your heart, and do not rely
on your own insight." (Proverbs 3:5,* NRSV)

God, this awful pain has separated me from trusting—trusting
myself, this marriage, and I am ashamed to say, even you.

When trust dies, it's like trying to build a skyscraper
without a scaffold.

There can be no going up from here, no future;
no possibility, no dreaming.

My heart has left my body and my soul also.
Judas killed himself but not his spirit.
Who will roll the stone away from the tomb
of my unforgetting?

Lord Jesus Christ, gate of all righteousness,
you are all-powerful, all-knowing, and universally present.

I need you to pull off something great in my life!

I can't take anymore of this sameness,
this conspiracy of degradation,
the constant belittling without a cause.

You have given me talents, gifts, abilities, and insight;
I am tired of being a symbol, an auxiliary to the main event,
a gala without a venue, a breath without a destiny.

The visions you have poured into me are bursting at the seams
of my hope, my patience, my sanity, and my confidence.

God, when will it be my turn to shine?

*"And will not God give justice to his chosen ones who cry
to him day and night? Will he delay long in helping them?
I tell you, he will quickly grant justice to them. And yet,
when the Son of Man comes, will he find faith on earth?"
(Luke 18:7-8, NRSV)*

6.

Lord, most excellent source of grace continuity
charity and laughter.
Right now, I don't know where you are.
I don't know where to go.
My stomach is bloated with regret and remorse.
Why can't I ever get it right—my marriage?

When will you come and help me?
Why do I feel so condemned, so worthless?
If I could just hear you speak my name, it would be enough.
Then I could sleep through the night, eat without nausea,
speak without offending, and return to the path
that leads to wholeness. Amen.

I am a prodigal with no sense of direction,
no compass, no navigator.
Nothing to show me the way home.
Please come and find me.
I don't want to die here.
Help me to live again.
Amen.

Gateways to Enchantment

"Blessed are the eyes that see what you see!" (Luke 10:23, NRSV)

1.

Lord Jesus Christ of Calvary,
Please do the miraculous in my life
through my purpose
with my finances
in my body
in my family

with my time
when I travel
in my relationships
in my leadership
and when I pray for the sick,
the troubled, the lost, the insane, or the deeply wounded.
Amen.

2.

They will call on my name,
and I will answer them.
—*Zechariah 13:9* (NRSV)

Come, Lord Jesus Christ,
Eternal Son of the Creator
Jewel of Golgotha
Fire of Pentecost
Come quickly.
Come fully.
Come in compassion.
Come with healing.
Come and raise me beyond my brokenness
that I too may serve the Lord of hosts.
To you alone do I call
The only great "I am"
The holy God of Israel and all nations
Come, Lord Jesus.
Come, blessed Sacrament.
Come ever-flowing Spring of life.
Come, holy Comforter.
Come, perpetual Sacrifice.
Come, mystical Trinity.
Come and reign in me both now and forever.
Amen.

3.

Lord Jesus Christ, Son of the living God,
worthy of all reverence, adoration, and devotion,
show me what I am holding on to that pushes you away.
Show me, and then give me the loving faith to trust
your love and let go of it; all of it.
I am listening for your voice . . .

[Spend some time in silence, then conclude:]

Thank you, God, our Holy Spirit, for making
these things known to me.
I renounce them all in expectation of the all-surpassing love
of Jesus Christ,
who heals me of all the disease in my life. Amen.

4.

I believe Abba is preparing to open the windows of heaven
and pour blessings into my life more wonderful
than I can conceive.
I am both ready and thankful to receive new life
in the name of the Lord Jesus Christ:
New health, enthusiasm, clarity, abundance, and peace.
My soul is open to the refreshing of the Lord,
my mind and my heart also.
Today let there be a manifestation. Today may I know freedom.
Today may Jesus be real to me.
Amen.

5.

Today my prayer to heaven is that I may be more completely
filled with the fullness of the presence of Yahweh. Amen.

6.

Holy God of compassion,
The dark shining of your presence summons me.
Yet you are the God beyond all knowing.
The tears of your passion bring desire to my soul.
Lead me to the gateway beyond the deep midnight.
Let the hush from your tabernacle make known to me your
infinite glory.
Woo me with the enchantment of your song.
Gentle me with the breath of your utterance.
Carry me away with the wings of your promise.
Endue me with the scent of heaven.
Restore my soul.
Let it happen now, Lord.
Let it be today.
Amen.

7.

Seek the LORD *while he may be found,*
call upon him while he is near.
—Isaiah 55:6 (NRSV)

Lord, you inhabit the realms of eternity and time.
You cause the ruminations of the universe.
Yet your footsteps pass through my remembering.
When my hope crumbles, you open the sky.
When my laughter fades; you bathe me in new beauty.
You kiss away my sadness and torment the devil.
You establish the meaning of my life.
You cause the movement of the sun and the stars.
You empty my pail of sorrow.
Hallelujah!

*Evening and morning and at noon I utter my complaint
and moan, and he will hear my voice. (Psalm 55:17, NRSV)*

Lord, Jesus Christ, Son of the living God,
let me now reach beyond the many veils woven for me
by sin, doubt, and the grave.
To you do I call. To me you send the answer.
Together we are one. Wonderful. One.
Hallelujah.

8.

Most holy God of all righteousness,
be glorified in the earth, worshipped and adored
in your sanctuary, and obeyed by your servants.
Rise in my soul. Dominate my thoughts.
I feel myself shutting down, diminishing, lost.
Close the gates to the torment of my past.
Awaken within me a fresh sense of purpose,
an excellent personality, new character.
Lord, only you can cause me to walk regally in holiness.
Cast all my fears far from me.
Wash me in piety. Baptize me into the glories of your joy.
Flood me with your divine light, and give me power to crush
the head of the serpent. In the mighty name of Jesus. Amen.

9.

Through you, we push down our foes. (Psalm 44:5, NRSV)

Holy Spirit, as you call me to the sanctity of rest; rest in me.
As you teach my soul again the rhythm and balance
of breathing, breathe in me.
As gently I embrace the mortality that I feared,
help me to live for the rest of my life. May I be given
the wings of self-love to carry me to new understandings.

Let there come such a stirring within me to worship the Lord
that I am ablaze with gratitude.
I want to walk in the integrity of my apostleship.
Help me to live with godly enthusiasm,
unconditional generosity
and peace that surpasses understanding. Amen.

10.

Today I call you Illaya (the exalted one).
May you be exalted in all the earth.
May every people and language and generation
exalt your name forever.
Let us worship the Lord, Illaya, the great wonder.
The all-inclusive mystery.
The ever-present majesty. The glory of heaven.
Let our thoughts, our tears, our memories exalt the almighty,
holy One. Lord, you are beyond my thoughts and in my heart.
You are greater than all knowledge and understanding.
I open my life to your wisdom, your perfection.
Lord of eternity, take possession of me totally;
that I may be shaped by your purpose,
subject to your teachings, and liberated by your truth.
I am wholly yours.
A devotee without reservation.
The spouse of your return.
A willow in the wind of your infinite grace.
You are to me forever Illaya
Illaya
Illaya
Illaya.

11.

Today, most holy and ancient gateway to the light,
I open my soul to receive new life, new breath,
the breathing of the Lord.
The whole universe inhales, and I am uplifted; exhales,
and I am restored.
The gates of shalom open wide before me.
Welcomed by the light I enter, I surrender, I am illumined,
I am healed, I am reborn by the life of God.
I am become the manifestation of divine enchantment:
Inebriated.
Transformed.
Unleashed by the light:
Enraptured by dreams and visions.
Pursued and overtaken by the favor of the Lord.
I fear no evil.
Hallelujah.
Amen.

12.

O LORD, our Sovereign,
  how majestic is your name in all the earth!
You have set your glory above the heavens.
—*Psalm 8:1 (NRSV)*

May my very soul ascend in a holocaust of praise
to the glory of your holiness.
Sanctify me with your passion.
Rebuke me in your justice.
Only always remain with me and within me.
I have loved and been loved imperfectly . . .
Given and received the mess of human weakness . . .
Made vows and despised them . . .
until in your compassion
you peeled away the illusions.

Kissed healing into my wounded places.
Sent a burst of glory into my vision.
Humiliated the accuser of my soul.
Nurtured my possibility.
Sang songs of love over my marriage bed.
Defeated poverty, lack, and disease.
Flooded my heart with hope
my eyes with purpose
and my desire with enchantment.
Thank you, Lord.
Thank you.
Thank you very much.